Whitetail Quest

Hunting Wisdom Library™

NORTH★AMERICAN★HUNTING★CLUB

MINNETONKA, MINNESOTA

WHITETAIL QUEST
Edited by Tom Carpenter

Printed in 2011.

Jen Weaverling
Managing Editor

Jenya Prosmitsky, Kate Opseth
Book Design & Production

Special thanks to: **Mike Billstein, Terry Casey, Janice Cauley and Heather Koshiol.**

8 9 10 11 12 / 13 12 11
© 2006 North American Hunting Club
ISBN 10: 1-58159-286-8
ISBN 13: 978-1-58159-286-3

North American Hunting Club
12301 Whitewater Drive
Minnetonka, Minnesota 55343
www.huntingclub.com

CONTRIBUTING WRITERS

Charles J. Alsheimer, Todd Amenrud, Scott Bestul, Tom Carpenter, Gary Clancy, Neil Dougherty, Tom Fegely, Brad Herndon, Gordy Krahn, Dave Maas, Bob Robb, Bryce M. Towsley and Dr. Grant Woods

PHOTO CREDITS

Charles J. Alsheimer 8, 14, 26, 34 (right), 52 (top), 67 (bottom), 90, 106, 116, 119 (bottom), 120, 122, 125 (top), 131, 135 (bottom), 147, 153, 154 (bottom); **Todd Amenrud** 59, 60, 61, 154 (top), 155; **Mike Barlow** (Windigo Images) 56 (bottom). **Scott Bestul** 53, 64, 66; **Tom Carpenter** 43, 56 (top), 75 (bottom), 84, 113 (top). **Tim Christie** 34 (left); **Gary Clancy** 10, 13, 22, 23, 35 (top), 37, 40, 46 (bottom), 49, 91, 92; **Judd Cooney** 39, 96; **Mark Drury** 17; **Tom Fegely** 138, 149, 150, 151. **Michael Francis** 52 (bottom), 97 (left); **Brad Herndon** 146, 148; **Don Jones** 6, 16, 18, 20, 24, 42, 44, 58, 68, 70, 83, 85, 99, 101, 107, 111; **Mitch Kezar** 33; **Bill Kinney** cover, 25, 30, 36, 46 (top), 48, 50, 67 (top), 69, 78, 97 (right), 100, 102, 108, 125 (bottom); **Gordy Krahn** 75 (top), 130; **Lance Krueger** 5, 10, 11, 35 (bottom), 45, 47, 54, 62, 72, 73, 76, 86, 88, 89 (right), 94, 98, 104, 110, 112, 113 (bottom), 114, 126, 137, 142, 152; **Dave Maas** 141 (middle right); **NorthCountry Whitetails** 115, 117, 118, 119 (top), 123, 128, 129, 133, 135 (top), 139, 140, 141 (top middle); **Mark Raycroft** 67 (middle); **Bob Robb** 7, 27, 28, 29, 87, 89 (left); **Ron Spomer** 32; **Bryce M. Towsley** 79; **Mark Werner** 1, 19, 74, 80, 81.

MAP ILLUSTRATIONS

Frank Peak 144, 145; **Larry Sickmann** 38, 124.

Table of Contents

INTRODUCTION

As whitetail hunters, we're all on a personal quest of some sort. And no matter where we're at, each stage offers a good and worthwhile focus.

For the beginner, just seeing deer in the wild may be reward enough. Getting a shot, or close to it, is a heart-pounding bonus worthy of babble and excitement back at camp. Being there and doing it —just hunting—is the reward.

After a couple years in the whitetail woods, a burning desire for success kindles in a hunter's heart. Sooner or later, that success happens. Who could ever forget every detail of his first deer? The day, the feeling and the elation all live on forever.

Then the goal often turns to "filling out" ... using this growing hunting confidence and these new-found deer hunting skills to put a lot of venison on the table and maybe some antlers on the wall. Notched tags equal big success. Many of us stay in this stage for a long time, and there are no apologies needed for that!

Some hunters then start turning to big bucks as whitetail hunting's ultimate challenge and reward. This is fine too, as long as we actively take part in herd management by shooting antlerless deer when game departments call for it.

As we start aging a little bit and the old treestand becomes a little harder to get in and out of, our aim may shift again—to a simple appreciation of being out in whitetail country, hunting hard and feeling good. Sure, those of us at this stage still love to hunt and shoot deer ... but we don't gauge our self-worth on filled tags or inches of antler. At each of these stages, getting better at this challenging art of whitetail hunting is embedded at the heart of the journey. That's where this book, *Whitetail Quest*, comes in. Here is hands-on, in-the-woods, real-world, no-fluff whitetail hunting expertise to help you become an even better deer hunter. And you will.

In "Deceive Them," you will improve your tactics for foiling a whitetail's astounding eyes, ears and nose. In "Hunt Them," you will expand your knowledge of essential hunting strategies and techniques. And in "Grow Them," you will absorb a wide variety of invaluable insights on managing your hunting land for an optimal herd ... and big bucks.

Oh yes. There is one more stage to the deer hunter's lifelong journey. It comes back to just being there again, outside in nature's quiet and magnificence, with just the chance to see one of its best and most beautiful creations—a white-tailed deer. Shooting may be secondary, or even unnecessary.

We're all at some point of this deer hunting journey, and may we arrive at that last stage with good health and the ability to make it out to the forests, woodlots, fields, prairies, hills, ridges, mountains, marshes, swamps or wherever else the whitetail leads you. In the meanwhile, there's a lot or hunting to be done. So let's make the most of our own *Whitetail Quest*, whatever it may be.

Tom Carpenter
Editor, North American Hunting Club Books

Tom

PART I

Deceive
Them

The first step to consistent deer hunting success—and getting big bucks—is deceiving the whitetail's eyes, ears and, especially, its magnificent nose. Ignore these ultimate defenses and you will pay. Attend to every hunting detail—from the passive techniques of sitting perfectly still or keeping the wind in your face to the aggressive tactics of using sexual attractant scents or rattling antlers—and you will find success in the whitetail woods. The whitetail is an extreme animal, so you need to practice extreme deception ... every minute of every hunt of your whitetail quest.

HOW TO SIT STILL

At its core, whitetail hunting is simple: Stay put, and eliminate unnecessary movement.

BY GARY CLANCY

*I*n his younger days, my father-in-law was a one-man deer drive. The sun would just inch over the crest of the limestone bluffs guarding the banks of the Mississippi River on opening morning, and already Dick would be vacating his morning stand. First he'd head over to check on John; then Larry up on the sidehill stand would get a visit; then Bob over on Nel's Knob; then Little Gary by the windmill; then Jerry and his boys up the Chimney Rock valley. Sometimes he even came tromping up the valley we called Crazy Man to see if all the shooting he had heard was coming from my old pump gun.

Yes sir, Dick moved a lot of deer all right, but he rarely saw one, much less shot one. In fact, the last one anyone can remember was a deer that had the misfortune of happening upon Dick one morning as he was "answering nature's call," which is about the only way you were going to get Dick to sit still for more than a few seconds in a row. We were all mighty grateful for Dick's inability to sit on stand for more than an hour at a stretch. Even during slow times, we always had hope of action as long as Dick was on the move.

But time has a way of catching up with all of us, and as the seasons added up, Dick's knees and bad hip complained so bitterly after a day of tromping the hills and "checking on the boys" that even the one-man deer drive was forced to become a stand hunter. Larry and I built Dick a cozy ground blind out of deadfalls out behind Earl's barn. For all of the 30 years we have hunted this piece of ground, bucks in search of does or perhaps slinking away from other hunters, cross an open area at this spot between two steep draws. It's one of those magical places where you know that if you sit long enough, a buck will show.

On opening morning, I happened to be hunting from a treestand on the opposite ridge from one of those timbered draws. We had a nice blanket of snow that year, and when the sun came up and bathed the far slope in the soft, yellow light of a new day, I saw a blob of orange gyrating on the far ridge. It was Dick. The temperature was in the single digits that morning, and my father-in-law, all 240 pounds of him, was on his feet doing a little jitterbug to get some heat generated. Dick never saw the doe that came charging out of the opposite draw in an effort to elude the panting buck hot on her tail. But the doe saw Dick doing his little dance, veered hard right, made a big loop and dove back into the same draw that she had just exited, with the super-charged buck in hot pursuit. Dick sat down a few minutes later, and I breathed a sigh of relief. I really wanted Dick to get a buck; all of us did. Larry and I figured he had a good chance now that he was forced to sit instead of roam. But just sitting, even in a good spot, is not enough.

Ten minutes after the buck and doe had disappeared, movement from the blob of orange again caught my attention. Because the V-shaped blind Larry and I had built was open on the end facing my direction, binoculars gave me a good view of what was going on inside the blind. Dick was pouring a cup of coffee from his ever-present Thermos. Fifteen minutes after that, it was time

Even hunters nestled in high treestands need to sit still and then move only in slow motion in order to avoid detection by sharp-eyed whitetails. Experienced hunters know that Eastern deer, especially, are learning to look up for danger.

for some of Grandma Babe's carrot cake. Ten minutes later, Dick was back on his feet stomping from side to side. Then he sat down and had some cookies. And so the morning went—the orange blob in nearly constant motion. I never told Dick about the doe and the buck, or the really big buck that tried to cross the knoll at mid-morning before spotting Dick fidgeting in the blind. That buck, too, sneaked out of sight as only a whitetail can sneak. When the noon whistle sounded in the little town of Plainview a few miles away, I wasn't surprised to see Dick pick up his folding stool and gun and head back toward camp.

At camp that evening, Larry and I encouraged Dick to give the deadfall stand another try the next morning, but he would have none of it. "I sat there all morning and never saw a deer," he told us. "Why would I want to waste another morning there?" I bit my lip; no sense rubbing salt in the wound.

I use my father-in-law as an example of what I consider to be the biggest misconception in stand hunting. There is a big difference between sitting in one location for a long time and sitting still. You are much better off sitting still in one spot for only one hour, than you are staying put on stand the entire day but never really being still.

STATUES ON STAND

Of the three senses upon which a whitetail depends for survival—smell, hearing and sight—his vision is the least acute. In fact, most of us can see better than a whitetail can. So do most of the other game animals we hunt. A whitetail cannot pick you off from an honest mile away like a pronghorn can. Unlike that old longbeard answering your yelps, or the flock of mallards cautiously making one last pass over your blind, a whitetail cannot readily distinguish color. And while a fox, coyote or crow can easily and instantly recognize you as "homo sapien" by your shape alone, the whitetail has no such ability. It was not the blaze orange coveralls that gave Dick's position in the ground blind away that opening morning, nor was he picked off from yonder ridge or identified as danger merely by his shape. Movement alerted the doe and, later, the big buck to Dick's presence. A whitetail is a master at detecting movement. Nature has seen to it.

While our own retinas are dominated by cones, which are color receptors, a whitetail's retinas are short on cones but long on rods, which are light receptors. In fact, rods are nearly 1,000 times more light-sensitive than cones. This, along with the reflective pigment called "tapetum," which is what makes a deer's eyes glow in your headlights, and the fact that a whitetail's pupil gathers nine times the light of our own is what gives the whitetail outstanding vision in poor light. These adaptations also give the whitetail excellent peripheral vision and an uncanny ability to detect motion.

Each of those side-mounted eyeballs can scan nearly 180 degrees, which means that a whitetail can detect movement everywhere but directly behind. When a whitetail looks ahead, it has binocular vision and excellent depth perception covering a 90-degree span. Looking to the sides, the whitetail employs monocular vision which results in poor depth perception. And as if all of that is not enough to deal with, a whitetail can see ultraviolet (UV) light, which is beyond the spectrum of our eyes.

Wash your hunting clothes in any popular household laundry detergent, and to a whitetail that clothing now glows.

So treat all of your hunting clothing with UV Killer and wash clothes only in detergent that does not have brighteners added. Call it cheap insurance.

Do You Have the Grit for an All-Day Sit?

There are two times during the season when sitting on stand all day dramatically increases your odds of seeing deer. One is the rut. Anytime bucks are traveling in search of does, running scrape lines or tending estrous does, I sit all day if my schedule allows. When the rut is in progress, that buck of a lifetime could just as easily show up at high noon as at the more traditional hours of first and last light. In fact, my hunting log shows that while my rut-hunt buck sightings are highest during the early-morning hours, the three-hour period from 11 a.m. until 2 p.m. runs a close second. This midday period also results in nearly twice as many sightings as does the afternoon/evening period.

The other factor that will encourage me to do an all-day sit is hunting pressure. This normally occurs during the first weekend of the firearms season. At no other time are there as many hunters afield, and all of that activity disrupts a buck's normal pattern. I've lost count of the number of deer that I have killed at midday during the first day or two of a firearms season. Most of these deer were bounced loose by hunters either leaving the woods for a lunch break, or returning to their stands after a midday break. Some had slipped through drives being conducted by other hunters in the area.

Staying warm is the biggest physical challenge to sitting all day. It's tough enough to stay put on a stand all day when you are comfortable. I've sat all day when the temperature never rose above zero at least a dozen times over the years. On one of those days, the high temperature was a bone-numbing 15 below. And while I will not go so far as to say that I was comfortable on those occasions, I was able to stick it out thanks to proper clothing, plenty of warm liquids and frequent snacks.

But it is not the physical part of an all-day sit that defeats most hunters, it is the mental game. Confidence in your stand site is crucial. Once you begin to doubt that you are sitting in the best location for the current conditions, you are finished. I rarely attempt an all-day sit in a stand that I have not pre-scouted and selected myself. Once I lose confidence in a stand, I move to another site. Once I lose confidence I also lose concentration, and once my concentration is gone, I'm going to begin to fidget and to forget about moving in slow motion. In short, I'm going to get sloppy.
—*Gary Clancy*

Matinee seating can provide some of the day's best hunting ... if you have the grit to stay put all day.

COMFORT COUNTS

You can't sit still if there is a branch stub stabbing you between the shoulder blades or a root jabbing you in the behind. Whether you hunt from a tree-stand or on the ground, do everything you can to make yourself as comfortable as possible. When hunting aloft, make sure that you can lean back against the trunk in a comfortable position. If I know that I am there for the long haul, I tie an extra seat cushion around the trunk on which to rest my back. And speaking of seat cushions, if you look in the back of my pickup anytime during the deer season, you will find a half-dozen of them. That is how important I think it is to have something soft to sit on.

Even with a good backrest and butt-pad, I can sit on the ground for only about an hour before my lower back begins to complain or my legs cramp up. I prefer a light, portable folding stool propped up against the side of a substantial tree or snuggled into a natural blind such as the branches of a deadfall.

THE SLO-MO RULE

We live in a society that places a premium on speed and efficiency. Close that deal by noon; get that letter cross-country by the start of business hours tomorrow; replace the old computer with a newer, faster model; dash crosstown to catch your son's basketball game and then drive like a mad-man in the other direction for your daughter's piano recital, all with a cell phone stuck to your ear, of course. Go, go, faster, faster—that is the American way. Is it any wonder that when we finally get a weekend to escape to the places that the whitetail calls home, we find it difficult to slip into slo-mo?

It takes conscious and constant effort to do everything in slo-mo. It is our nature to reach quickly for that candy bar, to snap our heads around when we hear a twig break, to lunge for our binoculars when we spot movement in the thicket. But if you think each time before you move, instead of just reacting, slo-mo will eventu-ally become a reality. And if you are fortunate enough to hunt more than just a weekend or two

each season, making each move in slo-mo will become second nature to you.

THE 300-YARD RULE

Math is not my strong suit, so these numbers might be a tad off. I figured one time that if there are between 20 and 40 deer per square mile in the area that you hunt—which are common numbers these days—and assuming that those deer are not evenly distributed over the entire 640 acres, which they never are, and assuming that you have selected your stand carefully, putting you right in the heart of the greatest deer density within that square mile, there should be a deer within 300 yards of your stand right now. I use those numbers and that image to keep myself from getting sloppy on stand and to keep myself from giving up on a stand too soon. It works for me. See how it works for you.

Unless you are able to sit still for long periods of time on the stand, chances are good you will never get close to a nice buck like this.

Beating Boredom on Stand

Hey, I enjoy a spectacular sunrise as much as anyone. And yes, I get a kick out of watching squirrels chase each other up and down oak trees, nuthatches walking upside down on tree trunks, blue jays complaining about everything in sight and a wedge of geese riding a stiff north wind to someplace I've never been. But I have to admit, sitting on a stand all day can get mighty boring sometimes. Here are some tips for beating boredom.

• Rattling and calling really help to "keep me in the game" during long stints on stand. Not only do both require physical action, but I know that during that 15 minutes after I tuck away the grunt call or hang up the horns, a buck could be slipping my way. Rarely does a half-hour pass that I do not reach for my grunt call. The same is true with rattling. I work the horns frequently during my stints on stand. Early and late in the season, I confine my rattling activities to just tickling the tines. But from late pre-rut right through the breeding phase of the rut, I rattle loudly and often.

• Using a decoy has really helped me beat boredom on stand. When you have a buck come into a decoy, even if you decide to pass on it, just watching the animal interact with the fake is an adrenaline rush that never fails to keep me alert for hours.

• I'm big on using deer scents (See "Using a Buck's Nose Against Him" on page 31). By laying down a long scent trail on my hike into the stand, I am encouraging any buck that crosses my trail to follow the scent to my stand. That means that I will see more deer, and I don't know anyone who gets bored on stand when he is seeing deer.

• Many hunters read while on stand. The ones I know read paperback books that slip easily into a pocket when a deer shows up. Most of them read a page, take a careful look

Some hunters pass the long hours on the stand reading, pausing between pages to have a good look around.

around, then read another page.

• Alternate standing and sitting, but don't forget to do it in slo-mo. The longest days I've ever spent on stand have been in box blinds in Saskatchewan where sitting was the only option.

• Carry plenty of food and water or a hot beverage in a Thermos if it is really cold. I like to take a couple of special treats, say a honey bun or two for instance. Then I reward myself at certain hours with that special treat.

—*Gary Clancy*

WHEN ONLY THE BEST WILL DO

Smart stand placement yields big bucks.

BY BRYCE M. TOWSLEY

Most hunters scout for deer sign and then hunt where they find it. After all, they reason, it makes sense to place your stand where deer are making the most tracks.

I suppose it does, if you are looking for little bucks.

If you want big bucks, you need to hunt where there aren't many deer. Most hunters tend to concentrate their efforts where they find the most deer sign, not realizing, or perhaps not caring, that most of that sign was made by does and small bucks. This will, of course, lead them to conclude that there are no good bucks around. The truth is that anywhere deer are hunted, even on public lands that see a lot of hunting pressure, some bucks make it past that critical first year. They mature out of the "kid-like" foolishness of a young buck while gaining an education.

If a buck is destined to make it through many more years, he will start acting differently than the rest of the herd. As a rule, the older a buck gets, the more pronounced this behavior becomes. If you are to have any reasonable chance of shooting one of these deer, you must do as they have surely done; adopt the habits of a loner.

Older bucks do not act the same as other deer. They shun company; they live in fringe areas, and when hunting season is open, they avoid prime feeding areas or deer concentrations during daylight hours. Old bucks grow old because they know that their No. 1 predator, man, will be waiting there.

They might act differently than other deer, but older bucks still have to eat, and most of them are desperate to grab their share of the rut's once-a-year opportunity for female companionship. But they have learned to do it on a different schedule than the rest of the herd; usually, well after dark.

The strongest advantage that hunters have in the early season is that a buck will instinctively feed heavily to put on enough weight to get through the impending rut and survive the upcoming winter. During the rut, the instinct to procreate dominates all other activity. The resulting impatience can cause a buck to make mistakes. You must do what you can to cash in on those mistakes.

HUNT TRAVEL CORRIDORS

Most good bucks hide away during daylight hours where they are least likely to be bothered. Your best chance to intercept them is to hunt travel corridors between food sources (which also attract does) and those "safety zones." To find them, remember that those bucks are living solitary lives, and while they might visit the rest of the herd at night, they will not be traveling or bedding in the same location as the rest of the deer. Look for the thickest, nastiest, most inaccessible and

more than his nose. He will usually travel into the wind and almost always approach feeding or bedding areas from downwind, so consider this when scouting.

STAGING AREAS

Look for staging areas where a buck will pause to wait for darkness if he leaves his bed early. These will have thick cover, good escape routes and a food source. While he might feed in prime locations during the dark of the night, that doesn't mean he will only feed there. In early fall, bucks feed almost constantly and will wait in staging areas where ferns, mast, apples or whatever else are available. Often, these areas will contain rubs and scrapes from previous seasons as well as rubs from this year, indicating that he often spends time there.

UTILIZE CHOKE POINTS

Funnels in travel corridors are excellent locations for stands. Place your stand on a choke point or bottleneck along the travel route, as near to the buck's bedding area as possible. You are trying to catch him in the morning, just before he enters his sanctuary and beds for the day. By hunting close, you might intercept him soon after he leaves his bed in the evening. The smartest bucks do neither in daylight and are harder to kill. But most bucks will occasionally stretch things by leaving or entering their hiding places a little early or late.

inhospitable cover that you can find within reasonable distance of food sources or doe concentrations. Just remember, a "reasonable" distance from prime food sources might be measured in miles instead of yards.

When scouting for travel routes, keep in mind that sign left by a big buck will be subtle, because he is just passing through and spending as little time on these trails as necessary. He will probably make a small scrape or two, and a few trees might show rubs. But don't look for those torn-up places that make any hunter's blood pump faster. Instead, concentrate on looking for his tracks. They should be larger than those of other deer in the area and almost always set off by themselves.

A mature buck will most likely use corridors that provide good cover, even if it means traveling out of his way, and he will seldom travel on well-worn deer paths. Instead, look in the thick cover paralleling the well-used trails, on the downwind side when possible. There is nothing a buck trusts

Some of the best funnels are those formed by beaver dams. Bucks seem to be attracted to them, perhaps because they provide good cover, food and water. But I think that there's more to it than that. I can't resist checking out a beaver dam. If I know one is in the area, I am compelled to seek it out. And if I discover a new one in my wanderings, I go directly to it. I don't know why, exactly, but it is primitive and buried deep within me. I think it's the same with big bucks.

Because beaver dams form a natural barrier and are often located in a valley, the edges are natural travel corridors. This, coupled with their attraction, make them ideal locations for stands.

Mark's Mississippi River Monster

Mark Drury has all the proof he needs that hunting away from most of the deer sign is key to finding big bucks.

When Mark's brother Terry found a buck's hiding place at the end of a ¾-mile-long strip of river-bottom along the Mississippi River in Illinois. One end of the woods opened to cropland and contained numerous rubs, scrapes, tracks and other sign. At the other end there was nothing but a faint trail that was almost devoid of tracks, leading into an area that had grown into a jungle of brush and briars. Most hunters would set up on the abundant sign, but there was a track on that hint of a trail that was 7¼ inches long from tip to dewclaw.

It took a few days, but when the wind was finally right, Terry and Mark were in a tree on that faint trail, rattling horns and blowing a prototype deer call while they videotaped the results.

"After a sequence late in the afternoon, I looked to my right and there stood a 180-class buck at 20 yards," Mark said. "He came slow and cautious until he was right under us, looking for the bucks that he had heard fighting. When he failed to find them, he turned to leave, and I bleated to stop him at 12 yards. I stepped out on my stand to get a better angle, drew and released. By the time that I felt calm enough to trust my legs to climb down, it was too dark to trail him.

"I knew the hit was good," Mark said, "but in the morning we lost his blood trail after several hundred yards. We looked for hours, but couldn't find him. I was sick, thinking we had lost him.

"We started out to get help and almost

Well-known game call developer and calling champ Mark Drury of Outland Sports took this great Illinois buck by hunting a faint travel route that showed a big track.

tripped over him lying in a field 200 yards from the last blood."

The non-typical 195 ⅛-point (gross) Boone and Crockett Club buck was the first to fall to the new M.A.D. grunt-snort-wheeze call.

"I used the grunt-snort-wheeze first," Mark said. "Then I rattled hard and loud for about 45 seconds. The buck showed up within seconds."—*Bryce Towsley*

GETTING CLOSE

When you can, place your stand close to the bedding area, but be sure that you can approach and enter it without being detected every time you hunt from it. Usually, this means that you must have it at least 200 to 300 yards from where you expect the buck to be bedded. A stationary stand is better than a climber because it can be entered quietly. If the property is isolated or private, you might go in a few weeks before the season and hang some treestands. But on public land, the risk of theft is usually too great.

If I must take my stand out with me after the hunt, I use a climber. I locate trees that can be used with climbing treestands while scouting before or after the season. I'll bring in a stand then and climb the tree to check out the setup. Often, this reveals problems, such as brush in the shooting lanes, when there is still time to deal with them. When it comes time to hunt, it is imperative to set up and climb the tree quietly, particularly on the afternoon hunt when you are most likely to be close to the buck.

This strategy is predicated on the hope that the buck's sanctuary is far enough away from other deer and other hunters so that he will be a little late showing up in the morning or quick to leave in the afternoon. But it's important to get there before he arrives. If you can't be in the stand before shooting light in the morning, hunt somewhere else. The same in the afternoon: Try to be in place when the sun is still high.

You must watch your approach. Everybody who hunts knows enough to place his stand where the wind is blowing away from the deer. The mistake many hunters make, though, is allowing their scent to drift where the buck can smell them while they are walking to their stand. This sets off an alarm in any old buck's head. He might not know where you are when you are hunting, but he knows where you were headed. He is likely to arrange his exit strategy around this knowledge. Remember, he didn't get big by being stupid.

NOCTURNAL BUCKS

Sometimes bucks are so nocturnal that they simply will not leave their hidey-holes in daylight. If the sign that you see while hunting tells you that he is chasing does and feeding under the cover of night, you can sometimes slip into his bedding area while he is gone. A stand or two in his bedding area can work. Obviously, this is risky, but if it's your only option, what do you have to lose? Locate a few trees with that in mind during your post-season scouting and have the stands in place well in advance of the hunting season.

Being mobile is often the key to cornering a mature buck. If he feels pressure, he's going to re-route his travels to avoid it.

Beating a nocturnal buck is hard work. Get out early, control your scent and stay all day ... all for that magical moment when he finally appears.

You must get into place several hours before daylight to be safe. Practice obsessive scent control and remain quiet. Remember, the buck might be bedded very close or might be coming to bed very near the stand. Nobody said that it would be easy.

If you don't kill the buck early, you will have to stay on that stand all day and until after dark to make sure that he has left the area to avoid spooking him. Even then, you will have only one or two shots at it before he is on to you. It's not easy, it's all or nothing, but it can work.

Resist the urge to look around in any of these locations. You must do your scouting, locate stand placements and plan your approach routes during post-season scouting. Trust what you found then and get into your tree with the least amount of disturbance. Don't take one unnecessary step in the woods. It goes without saying that you will practice scent control, but anybody who thinks that he can eliminate every human scent molecule is a fool. You cannot poke around in a buck's living room without him knowing that you were there, so don't try.

If you change to these tactics, your success rate will drop from the days of hunting high deer concentrations and shooting younger bucks. But the quality of the bucks that you do take will improve. That's a trade-off that I can live with!

ODOR CONTROL

Beating deer hunting's number one problem.

BY GARY CLANCY

*I*f ever in the 30-plus years that I have spent hunting whitetails, I can honestly say that I patterned an individual buck, it was a giant, non-typical, Minnesota farm country buck that I nicknamed "Patches." He had the girth of a Hereford bull, the shoulders of an NFL linebacker, and twisted antlers with stickers and drop points going in every direction. Distinctive double "patch" throat markings gave him his name.

I first met the buck while checking mink sets along a drainage ditch one foggy morning just before Thanksgiving. He was bedded down in a little patch of scrub willows and yellowed canary grass not much bigger than a single-car garage. Because of the fog, I suppose, I was on top of the buck before he knew I was around. Like many whitetails do, he held his ground and let me pass. I would have, too, but I caught a glimpse of the top of that twisted mass of antlers sticking above the grass and stopped in mid-stride, not knowing exactly what I had seen, but that I had seen something.

When I took a step toward the chin-to-the-ground giant, he exploded from his hiding place like a Bouncing Betty landmine and went chugging down the top edge of the drainage ditch. I stood there clutching a fistful of #1½ longsprings. My heart, which had suddenly migrated from my chest to my throat, threatened to cut off the air

There are dozens of soaps, shampoos and sprays on the market designed to reduce human odor.

supply to my brain. I had never seen such a buck before and have seen only one of his caliber since.

The rest of that winter I hunted the country where I had seen the buck, hoping to catch another glimpse of him, but I did not. Even though I never laid eyes on him again that winter or spring, I knew he was still around. The day that I jumped him in the willows, I got a good look at his tracks. The imprints he left behind were longer, wider and sank deeper into the earth than any I had ever seen.

It was August when the buck and I crossed paths again. He stepped from a corn field into an adjoining field of soybeans near dusk and began nipping the new growth from the tops of the belly-high plants. I saw him several times during the next couple of weeks, always at dusk and always in that same soybean field. Then he disappeared. I would find his tracks often enough to know that he was still around, but I had no idea where to hunt him.

That changed in mid-October when the buck, feeling the ancient urging in his loins, began to take out his aggression on little and sometimes not-so-little trees. His rubs were not the passive removal of bark so often seen during pre-rut. When this buck put his horns to bark, the hapless victim was doomed to die. Some were even uprooted, probably because the branches became entangled in the buck's twisted maze of tines. I found a dozen rubs along the bank of Lime Creek and enough of the buck's tracks to complete the story.

The tracks always led south, so I figured the buck was only using the creek bank in the morning; probably his main route home after a night of carousing. I already knew that "home" was a 4-acre slough choked with a nearly impenetrable tangle of scrub willows, red osier and thick stands of cattails. The rubs were like milepost markers along a one-way highway.

On Halloween morning, I climbed a wind-ravaged, half-rotted weeping willow an hour before first light. The wind was light out of the northwest. I nocked a cedar arrow to the string on my Bear recurve and waited.

Dirty gray slowly replaced the black of night. A tight group of greenwing teal whistled up the creek. A pheasant croaked out a greeting to the new day. On the Vermedahl farm a half-mile away, I could hear the metallic slamming of hog feeder lids as the pigs did what pigs do best. And then I saw him, and the shakes set in so fast and so fierce that I thought I would fall from the tree. He was gently working an overhanging branch on a scrape about 100 yards to the north, almost lovingly caressing the tattered limb of the green ash on which he left his message in scent each day. Finished, he began walking my way.

I had such a bad case of buck fever that the

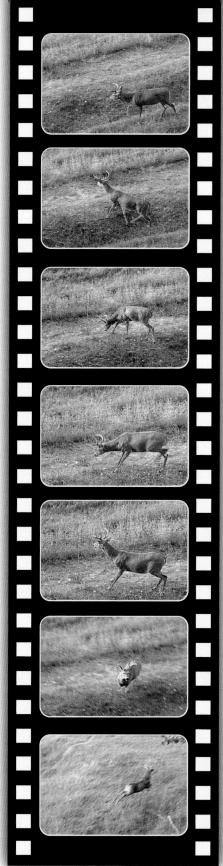

Things were looking good (top) on the first day of a Montana bowhunt that the NAHC team taped for television. But these photos from the video show what happened when this buck hit the foot-scent left by the hunter and cameraman.

odds of actually being able to draw and launch an arrow at all—much less one directed at the vitals of the buck—were slim; but who can say? Maybe, just maybe, by pure dumb luck, or some internal resolve to pull myself together at the last moment, I might have actually pulled it off. I'll never know. The buck was 40 yards away and coming steadily when he hit a wall. At first he just stared, then he raised his head and tested the fickle breeze that had shifted to the southwest and betrayed me. Like every big buck I've seen since, he trusted his nose without question. He turned and walked away. I never saw Patches again, nor did I hear of another hunter taking a giant buck from the area in the following years. My guess is that the big non-typical just lay down one morning and never got up again. Had it not been for my odor, he might have died from my arrow instead.

I do know this: If Patches and I had that same encounter along the banks of Lime Creek today, there is a better than 50-50 chance that he would not smell me. Odor control has come a long way since that morning. Today, bowhunters who are willing to look at odor control with an open mind and not write it off as a gimmick to sell products are a giant step ahead of the skeptics. Put today's odor control technology to work for you and you can beat bowhunting's No. 1 problem more often than not.

PERSONAL HYGIENE

Skip this step and you can forget the rest. Odor control starts with personal hygiene. Whenever possible, shower before each hunt using odor-free body soap and shampoo. If you can't shower, take a sponge bath and shampoo your hair. Up to 80 percent of the heat from our bodies escapes through our heads: that means sweat, and sweat means stink. There are dozens of unscented soaps and shampoos available, but make sure that the one you use rinses completely. If it does not, the soap scum it leaves on your skin and hair will most likely leave behind enough odor to tip off a buck to your presence.

Use an unscented anti-perspirant that is specifically designed for hunters. Many sporting goods stores sell them.

Breath odor cannot be eliminated, but you can dramatically reduce it by brushing your teeth and tongue with a combination of baking soda and salt, and then gargling with NO-ODOR. The active ingredient in NO-ODOR, antium dioxide, is the same chemical found in mouth rinses prescribed by dentists and oral surgeons to deal with gingivitis and other oral diseases. When using NO-ODOR as a mouth rinse, try not to swallow too much of it. NO-ODOR controls

body odor (and breath odor) by killing bacteria, and we need the bacteria in our stomachs to keep the digestive process working. I gargle about every hour when I'm on stand.

Odor-eliminating masks also work. However, I have not found one that is comfortable to wear in warm weather or does not cause glasses to fog over in cold weather. Chewing or sucking on a piece of apple will also help neutralize your breath.

There is no shortage of odor-free detergents on the market. Just make sure that the one you select rinses completely and does not have an ultraviolet brightener. Most common household detergents contain UV brighteners.

KEEPING IT SCENT-FREE

Don't use garbage bags for storing your clean clothing. The plastic smell of the bag will transfer to them. Use scent-free bags available from Hunter's Specialties and other sources, or store your clean, scent-free clothing in a clean cooler or large, scent-free tub with an airtight lid.

If you have a long hike to your stand, consider carrying most of your clothing so that you

Activated-charcoal suits (top) help neutralize human odor. Spray rubber boots (middle) with liquid odor eliminator on the outside, and use odor-absorbing powder inside. Apply powder to the inside of your cap (bottom) to eliminate the old stinky sweatband syndrome.

do not become overheated. But don't go right to your tree and then get dressed. No matter how careful you are, you will leave human odor behind where you stop to complete dressing. I stop 100 yards or more from my stand, take time to cool down completely, and then put on my final layers and slowly walk the rest of the way.

THE SCOOP ON BOOTS

It really doesn't matter if you wear leather or rubber boots as long as they are free of human odor. To accomplish this, spray the outside of both boots with a liquid odor eliminator and use an odor-absorbing powder, such as NO-ODOR II, on the inside of the boot. I have not had a chance to test any boots featuring activated-charcoal liners, but they should prevent foot odor from escaping. However, you will still need to use an odor-eliminating spray on the outside.

ODOR ELIMINATORS

Odor-eliminating sprays attack and neutralize the bacteria that cause us to stink. Most hunters buy a bottle, throw it in the back of the pickup and then spray some on their clothing before heading into the woods, assuming that they are now magically rendered scent-free. Far from it. Odor-eliminating sprays, which I prefer to call odor-reducing sprays, do work, but only when used as part of a total odor-control program.

I use these sprays on my boots as mentioned earlier, but the most critical application for them is after I reach my stand. When the weather is warm, no matter how slowly I walk to the stand, I perspire. After climbing into the stand, I partially strip and apply the spray to my underarms and groin and rub some into my scalp and hair.

Odor-reducing powders work differently than liquids. The best contain 75 percent unscented talc and 25 percent abscents crystals. If it does not specify at least 25 percent abscents crystals on the container, I would not waste my money. These crystals are actually a synthesized mineral developed by the diamond industry. Each abscents crystal will absorb 10,000 times its weight in the mole-

cules that cause body odor, making them nearly 10 times more efficient at trapping odor than activated charcoal. I rely heavily on powder, especially when it is too cold to comfortably use liquid spray.

Years ago, when Atsko first came out with NO-ODOR II, I tested it under extreme conditions. I wore the same pair of socks during a week-long archery elk hunt! Each morning, I powdered my feet and dumped some in my boots. At the end of the week, I passed the socks around to my three hunting companions for the "sniff test." They declared them free of any offensive odor, although the socks were nearly worn out from six days of hard climbing. That test made a believer out of me.

If you are like me, you probably have a favorite hunting cap. Smell the sweat band sometime. Whew! Applying powder to the inside of your cap will eliminate the old stinky sweatband syndrome.

SCENT-CONTROL CLOTHING

Scent-Lok, was the first odor-eliminating clothing to feature activated charcoal. I began wearing it the year it came out and was almost laughed out

Your boots make much contact with the ground, so take extra effort to eliminate scent on the day's footwear.

of several deer camps. Today, however, in those same camps, if there are 10 serious bowhunters, you can bet that seven or eight of them will be wearing Scent-Lok suits.

Using activated charcoal to neutralize odor did not originate in the hunting industry. Activated charcoal is being used around you every day. Chances are the water you drink is filtered through activated charcoal. And it is activated charcoal in the hood of your kitchen stove that removes fried fish odors. The military has activated charcoal suits designed to protect soldiers in the event of chemical warfare.

Gore-Tex has announced that it was introducing its own brand of fabric called Supprescent. And nearly every major clothing company, including such giants as Whitewater Outdoors, 10X and Browning, are offering products designed for the bowhunter with activated-charcoal liners. And activated-charcoal liners are not just for jackets and pants anymore. Caps, gloves, hoods, breath masks, packs, boots, you name it, will now be available with activated-charcoal technology.

Activated charcoal, which is full of little nooks, crannies and crevices, traps gases and molecules and prevents body odor from reaching the atmosphere. Picture a magnet sitting on your kitchen table—that magnet represents activated charcoal. Now dump metal shavings on the table. These metal shavings represent the stuff that makes us stink to a whitetail's nose. What happens? Yep, the metal shavings are attracted to the magnet and stick to it. That is what happens with activated charcoal and body odor.

Robinson Labs, makers of Scent Shield products, has introduced its own clothing line, called Scent-Blocker, and has made it easy for you to test its product with a simple scratch-and-sniff card. Lift the swatch of fabric, scratch and you will smell an odor. Now put the ScenTek material over the scented spot and sniff again. Nothing.

Remember, we are dealing with an animal in possession of an olfactory system so acute that it can easily analyze up to six different odors at one time, and so dependent upon its nose that one-third of its brain is devoted to olfactory functions. It is estimated that a whitetail's sense of smell is 25 times better than ours.

We are not at the point yet where we can be 100 percent odor-free—maybe we never will be. But, by using the technology that is available today, you can drastically reduce the chances of deer smelling you. In the old days, when a deer got downwind, you just kissed it goodbye. Today, thanks to advancements in odor control, eight times out of 10 a downwind deer will not smell me at all, or the odor that it does detect will be so minimal that it will write the smell off as either coming from too far away to be of concern, or to be lingering scent left behind by a long-departed hunter.

Drastically reducing human odor is not easy. Doing it right takes time and attention to detail. And, yes, you are going to have to spend some money. But from where I stand, the dollars that I spend on odor control are the best investment that I will make all season.

Somewhere there is another Patches. Our paths will cross someday. The buck might win again, but if he does, I'll bet it's not his nose that beats me.

Not only are you likely to see more deer when you pay attention to odor control, the ones you do see will offer better opportunities for a good shot.

THE SMELL OF SUCCESS

Everything you need to know about scents, and using them.

BY BOB ROBB

*I*t was prime time in Illinois, but too hot for white-tailed deer hunting. Mid-November temperatures soared near 80 degrees in Adams County, and while the bucks were rutting and moving, most activity was predictably occurring after dark. When I had a chance one afternoon to try something different and hunt the edge of a green field no one had hunted all season, I didn't hesitate.

My treestand was set in a bare oak directly opposite a freshly worked scrape. Before climbing into the stand, I found two well-tracked trails leading out of the adjacent, thickly brushed oak bottom. Both were 100 yards from my stand. "What have I got to lose?" I remember thinking. "I'll lay down a couple of scent lines and see what happens." Using some doe estrus scent, I did just that, terminating both draglines at the scrape 42 steps from my treestand.

When the giant buck appeared, I about passed out! There was plenty of daylight left for North American Hunting Club videographer Dan Larson to tape the action as the buck came out of the bottom, hit the scent line and worked his way to the scrape across from our stands. As he sniffed the scent wick I'd hung on the scrape's licking branch, I dropped the string on my bow. That buck remains my largest whitetail to date. His typical 10-point frame gross-scores 181 ⅜ Pope and Young Club points, and nets 173 ⅜ points.

Before going any further, let me cut to the chase. I've used scents off and on for more than two decades, with mixed results. There have been

times when they've worked magic, times when they've done nothing at all and times when I've seen deer hit a scent line and turn themselves inside out to get out of the area as fast as they could run.

That's a round-about way of saying anyone who believes all they have do to is spray themselves with a masking scent to cover human odor, fill the woods with the scent of a doe in heat and then get out the skinning knife, is in for a lot of grief. Scents can be a valuable tool in your hunting arsenal, but you have to use them wisely.

There's also much that people don't know about white-tailed deer behavior in general, and how and why deer react to scents in particular. The only way to find out for sure is to field-test a technique or scent product in your hunting area and see for yourself.

This huge Illinois 10-pointer followed a scent line to within shooting distance of the author's stand.

SCENT TYPES

There are five different types of scents: cover, food, curiosity, territorial and sex scents. Here's a quick look at each:

• **COVER SCENTS.** Also called masking scents, cover scents are used to prevent game from detecting human odor. They can be made from animal urine, plant extracts, etc. The most popular types used by hunters are coon and fox urine. Cover scents are useful all season.

• **FOOD SCENTS.** Appealing to a deer's sense of hunger, most food scents are made from natural plant derivatives. Most hunters use food scents native to their hunting area (apple scent in areas where apples are prevalent, for example); however, using a food scent not native to an area can also be effective. Food scents are best used during the early bow season and then again after the rut is over. Some hunters also use food scents as cover scents.

• **CURIOSITY SCENTS.** Odors other than food or another animal might also appeal to deer. These are curiosity scents, and it's anyone's guess which one will work and why. Anise, licorice and vanilla have been commonly used as curiosity scents. The only way to find out if a curiosity scent will work in your area is to test it yourself. They're best used during the early and late seasons, or on does during the rut.

• **TERRITORIAL SCENTS.** These can be urine or gland scents from white-tailed deer, which in effect tells other deer there's a visitor in the neighborhood. Often, the local herd members will take a strong interest in this fact and follow the scent to see if they can locate the "intruder." Using the tarsal glands of a freshly killed buck is a classic territorial-type scent that can, during the rut, elicit a challenge a rutting buck might have trouble resisting.

• **SEX SCENTS.** By far the most popular scent type used by deer and other big game hunters, sex scents are urine-based and collected from a doe in estrus. The plan is that during the rut when a buck smells this scent, he won't be able to resist and ends up following the smell past your stand. Sex scents are most effective during the rut.

While each of the five scent types have

their place, I've had the most success with cover and sex scents. Here's how I use them.

MASKING MY WAY

When choosing a cover scent, I prefer one made from animal urine instead of a plant derivative. If you use plant scent as a cover, use one native to your hunting area. I also use cover scents judiciously, believing a little goes a long way.

Red fox urine is my favorite masking scent. Deer seem to relax around it and sometimes even follow it. Next is coon urine, which some people theorize is the best for treestand hunting because coons climb trees. Regardless, I like to apply a little fox or coon urine to my boots (or a felt pad attached to my boots) as I walk to my stand. When on stand, I might place a scent wick with some masking urine on it in the tree with me, just in case the deer come downwind. I have friends who like to set up three masking scent wicks a few feet from their stand, one directly downwind, and the other two at 90-degree angles to the wind direction, again hoping these scents will help fool deer that get downwind.

One tip that seems to work when using boot scent pads is adjusting their position depending on how wet the ground is. If it's dry, I keep the pads on the bottom of my boots. If it's damp and the grass somewhat high, I rotate the pads to be

Using doe-in-estrus scent dispensed from a quality scrape dripper can influence bucks to check scrapes during legal shooting hours. Use red fox urine as a cover scent.

on the sides of my boots. On wet, grassy ground I might place the pads on top of my boot so the scent is left on the grass and not washed off into the wet ground. I also like to freshen the pads with more scent every 100 yards or so. Then, when I get to my destination, I use my boot pads as scent wicks around my stand.

SEX-SCENT STRATEGIES

I like using sex scents—a lot. However, I've seen both does and bucks run like the wind when encountering a scent line using a sex scent, so be forewarned that simply laying down a doe-in-estrus scent line isn't always the best thing to do. Again, gaining experience in your hunting area will tell you what works.

Generally speaking, I like to lay down a scent line using doe-in-estrus scents, then place a "scent bomb" in a couple of shooting lanes near my stand. I've killed several bucks passing through the thick areas I normally hunt that have stopped to smell the scent bombs. These bombs can be a commercial wick, a piece of felt or a couple cotton balls placed inside an empty 35mm film canister.

Territorial scents are also effective during the rut, and I've found them best employed on a wick set near my stand. One thing I like to do is use both a doe-in-estrus scent and buck territorial scent together, imitating a strange buck tending an estrous doe. Rutting bucks, and especially mature bucks, can't resist coming over to see who's messing with the local girls.

Doe-in-estrus scents also work well when hunting over scrapes. A scrape dripper, like the one made by Wildlife Research Center, that uses ambient temperature to release scent only during the day, is a great method for scrape hunting. The timing of the scrape dripper can teach a roaming buck that the only way he can see the doe visiting that particular scrape is to come to it during legal shooting hours and not after dark, when most scrapes are worked. Using a scent bomb over a scrape can also be dynamite.

Finally, I like to use doe-in-estrus scents when hunting with deer decoys, applying a small amount of lure to the decoy to give it added realism. Believe me, when a rutting buck has his interest piqued by a decoy, then circles downwind and gets a whiff of that estrous smell, he's going to come over to investigate!

Scent-Free is the Key

*E*xperienced hunters realize the importance of staying as scent-free as possible. When employing any type of scent product into your hunting, this is doubly important. To that end, before heading to my stand I follow this system: I wash my hunting garments in an unscented laundry detergent, preferably one that adds no UV-brighteners, then store my outerwear, including hat, gloves and face mask, in a heavy plastic bag; shower using an unscented soap and shampoo; liberally use an unscented deodorant and dress in clean clothing for the drive to the field. Once at my hunting site, I change into my hunting garments before walking to my stand at a pace that minimizes sweating. Then, before climbing into my stand, I liberally use a scent-eliminating spray or powder like Stealth Dust, covering everything.
—*Bob Robb*

USING A BUCK'S NOSE AGAINST HIM

A buck can use his nose to beat you. But you can also use it to beat him.

By Gary Clancy

Fishermen catch on quicker than most hunters. Muskie hunters know that muskies rely on their super-sensitive sight for survival, so they cast gaudy, easy-to-see lures. Bass fishermen, realizing that the bucket-mouth's lateral line will tune in on the slightest vibration, pitch lures that create a disturbance as they travel through the water. Catfishermen know that the best way to fill a stringer with channel cats is to appeal to the fish's incredible sense of smell and taste. But most deer hunters, even though they know that a whitetail's No. 1 warning system is its sense of smell, haven't a clue about using a buck's nose against him. If you're interested in seeing more deer, properly using scents can dramatically increase your odds. The biggest buck I've ever taken was a result of using deer scent.

My introduction to deer scents came in the early 1960s, when I spotted a small glass vial of "buck lure" on the shelf of my local fur buyer's shed. The price was $1, about the amount I received for a prime muskrat pelt. I used scents and lures to attract fox, coyotes, raccoons, mink and beavers on my trapline, so why not use them to attract deer? I bought the bottle of buck lure and have been using deer scents ever since.

My trapping background made it easy for me to accept using deer scents. Many hunters, however, view them as gimmicks designed for only one purpose; to separate hunters from their hard-earned greenbacks. In fact, I had used deer scents with good results for 15 years before I realized that many hunters considered them worthless. This attitude is still prevalent today. Some hunters are too set in their ways to give attractants an honest, unbiased try. I'm not going to waste my time trying to change this attitude. But I know that there are thousands of deer hunters reading this magazine who would like to know more about how to use deer scents and thousands more who have tried them without success. Those hunters are probably wondering if there is something they missed; a trick or a tip that might mean the difference between success and failure.

There are many ways to use deer scents, more than can be covered in one magazine article. But I will share the scent strategies that have proven most effective for me.

SCENT TRAILS

Scent trails, like most scent applications, are most effective during the rut, when amorous bucks spend a lot of time with their noses to the ground hoping to intercept the trail left by an estrous doe. I've had scent trails work before and after the rut, so I lay one down no matter what time of the year I am hunting.

There are two key points to remember when using a scent trail. One, the trail must be

Fake Scrapes

Not many years ago, mock scrapes were all the rage. Today, however, few hunters use them. Those who do seem to come up with big bucks each season. Coincidence? Maybe.

A mock scrape is nothing more than an artificial scrape. The idea is to get bucks to investigate your handiwork. Bucks might snoop around mock scrapes because of curiosity, perceived competition from another buck, or because they hope to get lucky and meet up with a doe. Who cares why? All I know is that mock scrapes work. Here are some keys to effective mock scrapes:

• Advertisers want their billboards displayed in high-traffic areas where they can grab the attention of every motorist cruising by. You don't see billboards stuck back in the woods along some dusty country road. The same applies to mock scrapes. If a buck doesn't see it, the scrape is worthless. A mock rub or two behind or off to the side of the scrape will also catch the attention of a passing buck.

• An overhanging branch is more important than the scrape itself. The branch is the real communication center. Every buck that visits your mock scrape will leave his scent on the

branch. Only the largest bucks are likely to actually work the scrape. Doctor the branch with a liquid, paste or gel containing forehead gland, preorbital gland, buck saliva, tarsal gland or a combination of any of these scents. This past season, I experimented with Wellington's new 24-Hour Scent Post and had good success with this long-lasting applicator, which I secured directly to an overhanging branch.

• Mock scrapes are most effective prior to the time when serious scraping activity begins. In my area, for instance, I know that dominant bucks begin making breeding scrapes around the middle of October, so I begin deploying my mock scrapes early in October. Think it doesn't get a big buck's attention when he finds that some upstart has been leaving scrapes on his home turf? Once the woods are littered with scrapes, the effectiveness of mock scrapes drops off dramatically.—*Gary Clancy*

consistent. If there are gaps in the trail of more than a few feet, deer will often lose interest. The second important point is that the amount of scent you deposit on the ground must remain constant for the entire length of the trail or increase the closer you get to your stand. If deer detect that the scent is growing weaker, they will turn around and follow it the other way.

Many hunters apply scent trails by dumping scent on the soles of their boots and then hiking to their stands. I've used this method myself, but it is a lazy man's alternative and leaves a lot to be desired. For one thing, it is impossible to regulate the amount of scent deposited with each step. The

first steps you take after spraying or pouring on the scent are always going to be the strongest. That's not what you want. And if you use your boot soles to lay down a scent trail, you are stuck with that odor on your boots the rest of the hunt. You apply scent to your tree steps, ladder, climber and stand platform. Not good. You run the risk of drawing unwanted attention to yourself when your boots smell like something of interest to deer.

Drag rags work. In the old days, when we had a bunch of little Clancys around the house, I used strips of worn-out but clean diapers, which I tied to a 5-foot length of baling twine. The diapers worked well because they absorbed a lot of scent, eliminating the need to stop often and refreshen. Commercial drag rags use high-tech materials that work on the same high-absorption principle as the diapers. Boot pads also work; just remember to stop and apply fresh scent every 30 to 50 yards. A better alternative is scent applicators that spray or drip scent with every step you take.

My favorite applicator is a tarsal gland or two. While wearing rubber gloves, peel the tarsal gland from a buck's inside knee on both of his hind legs. If the buck is in rut and the tarsals have a rank, musky smell, so much the better. I get mine from road-killed deer or from friends. After removing the tarsal gland, cut a slit in each gland so that you can tie a cord through the slit later. Deposit each tarsal gland in its own Zip-Loc bag. I put an ounce of doe-in-estrus urine into the bag with one of the tarsal glands; I leave the other as is, if the gland is pungent. If it is not, I add tarsal gland scent to the bag. When I hike to my stand, I drag them both behind me. I would like to think that when bucks smell the drag marks, they interpret the smell to mean that there is a buck hot on the trail of an estrous doe and if they want in on the action they had better get tracking.

Most instruction on how to lay down scent trails suggests beginning the trail 100 to 300 yards from the stand. I'm a believer in the long-distance scent trail. If it's a half-mile hike into my stand, I'll lay down a half-mile of scent. Maybe a buck won't follow scent that far, but it might get him coming in my direction. The whole reason for using a scent trail is to intercept bucks that would not otherwise come past your stand, so the longer the trail, the better the odds are of making contact with a buck.

One trick I use when laying down scent is to stop and freshen my scent each time I cut a deer trail on my hike into my stand. This way I have a better chance of grabbing the attention of bucks using the trail and giving them a good starting point.

SCENT POSTS

Scent posts serve two purposes. The first is to attract deer. A scent post allows scent to drift

Lay down a scent trail and you might intercept bucks that would not otherwise travel past your stand.

downwind to the deer. In my experience, deer need to be within 100 yards and downwind of the scent post before they get enough of a whiff to be led to the source, even closer if it is windy and the scent stream is scattered.

The second function is to stop deer and hold their attention long enough for a good shot. I consider this the most critical application of a scent post. Two years ago, I interviewed three bow-hunters who had taken Boone and Crockett Club bucks in the same season from the same county in western Wisconsin. Two of the three bucks were taken because of scent posts.

When bowhunting, I place my scent posts within 30 yards of my stand. You will see fancy diagrams when it comes to positioning scent posts for bowhunting, but the folks who draw these diagrams are, in my opinion, taking a very simple concept and complicating it. Place four to six

White-tailed bucks rely heavily on their noses to trail estrous does (left) and to keep track of what rival bucks are up to (right).

scent canisters or other applicators in a circle around your stand and you have covered all of the bases regardless of which direction deer approach from or what the wind does while you are on stand.

When hunting with a firearm, terrain and the range at which you feel confident shooting dictate how far away to place scent canisters. One November while filming a hunt, I placed a scent canister 225 yards from my stand. There was a 50-yard-wide slash through the thick Saskatchewan bush at that distance, and I knew that any buck crossing that cut would be gone before our camera could get on him. My hope was that bucks cutting across the opening would smell the scent and hold up long enough for the cameraman to do his job.

When a big 10-pointer cut across the opening at dusk, the only thing that saved us was that scent canister. As one can see on the video, the buck mills around trying to pinpoint the source of the tantalizing scent, giving the cameraman plenty of time to roll some tape before I make the

shot. Even if I had not been hunting with a cameraman, I would have put a scent post at that location. Don't be afraid to go the long-distance route when it comes to scent posts.

Hunters can choose from dozens of scent applicators designed for creating scent posts. All of these scent canisters, along with wicks and strips work, but none work better than the "scent bomb" that started it all. Every hunter I know who has used scent posts, began by using clean cotton stuffed in a clean 35mm film canister. I stress clean, because no matter what type of applicator you use, if you contaminate it with human odor, you have diminished the effectiveness of the scent. Always wear rubber gloves when handling scent or scent applicators.

Here are the key points to remember when deploying scent posts:
• Hang the scent bomb 3 to 5 feet above ground to keep the scent stream at a buck's nose level.
• Use doe-in-estrus urine and don't be a miser with the scent. Use at least 10 drops per set.

Juicing Up Your Decoys

Applying scent to your decoy will not attract more deer. However, it will cause the deer that approach your decoys to hang around longer, and the more time a buck spends parading around decoys, the more opportunity you have for a shot.

I use tarsal gland scent or a real tarsal gland on a buck decoy. No need to place the scent on the rear leg of the decoy, just tie a tarsal gland or a scent wick dipped in tarsal gland scent to a string and loop it around the decoy's tail so that the wick or tarsal hangs at knee level. A touch of forehead gland scent on the buck's head will also help.

When using a doe decoy, use the same string and scent-wick combination, but use doe-in-estrus urine or stick an acorn-sized glob of paste or gel to the decoy's rump.—*Gary Clancy*

Applying scent to a decoy will cause deer to hang around longer.

• Always hang scent bombs within range of your stand. It does no good to have a buck standing with his nose to the canister if you can't get a clear shot at him.

• Retrieve your scent applicator after the hunt. To make them easier to find in the dark, I attach a strip of reflective tape.

Using deer scent will not make up for sloppy hunting tactics. However, if you are a good hunter, properly using scents will allow you to see more deer, give you more time to observe the deer you see, afford you better opportunities for shots and add fun to an already enjoyable pursuit.

Take the time to carefully hang scent books within good bow range or surefire rifle range of your stand.

SCRAPE CONTROVERSY

To doctor or not to doctor.

BY GARY CLANCY

*I*t's been over two decades, but I can still see that buck coming down off the hardwood ridge as if it was this morning. To me he looked immense, although I'd later discover that his 8-point rack is 1½ inches short of the minimum requirement for the Pope and Young Club record book. What makes the buck so special isn't his size, but rather the fact that I took him as he stood in a scrape I'd doctored up with his demise in mind.

Give the old time machine a spin and there I am sitting in my stand on a Kansas river-bottom last November. My friend and outfitter, Jeff Louderback, had seen a big buck in the vicinity a few days before my arrival. The rut was winding down, but I found a big, hard-hit scrape, doctored it up and latched my treestand to a cottonwood to see what would happen. The buck, much bigger than the one I'd taken from a doctored scrape so many years before, was standing in that doctored scrape with his antlers working the overhanging branch when I released the string on my bow and sent an arrow through his lungs.

Spend as much time in deer camps around the country as I do and you're going to hear different

Doctoring a scrape will often make it more appealing to rut-crazed bucks on the move.

opinions on whether you should doctor a scrape. Some great hunters who've taken dandy bucks while hunting over scrapes are adamant about never going near the scrape itself, much less adding anything foreign to it.

I won't argue with these hunters. If you're satisfied with the results you're getting while hunting over scrapes, then who am I to tell you to change your ways? But if you, like I once did, find yourself spending long hours sitting over scrapes that never or rarely get visited while you're in attendance, then you might want to consider making one or more of those scrapes more appealing to bucks. The idea behind doctoring scrapes is to make them more appealing to bucks so they're more inclined to visit them more often than they do others.

Compare a doctored scrape to your favorite restaurant. My family and I live in a small town not far from a city of 80,000 people. There are more than 50 restaurants in that city and yet, more than half of the time when we go out to eat, we return to the same restaurant because it's our favorite. We like the food, the service, the cleanliness, the owner and his staff, so we return time

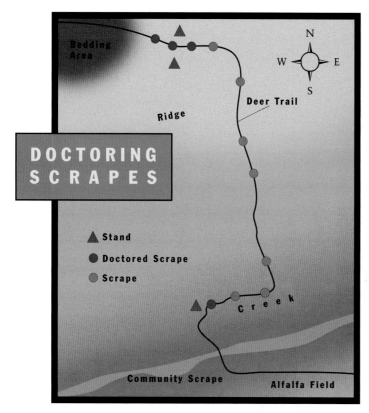

DOCTORING SCRAPES

Bedding Area

Ridge

Deer Trail

N
W E
S

▲ Stand
● Doctored Scrape
○ Scrape

Creek

Community Scrape

Alfalfa Field

Don't doctor every scrape along a deer trail. Your best spots for ambushing a buck are near his bedding area or at a funnel, like a shallow creek crossing.

didn't practice what I'd consider adequate human odor control while doctoring the scrape. If you leave human scent behind at the scrape, you have set a booby trap that's going to explode in your face, which is not the buck trap you'd intended. When I doctor a scrape, I'm paranoid about my human odor, so I wear rubber gloves, clean rubber boots and a Scent-Lok suit.

WHICH SCRAPES TO DOCTOR

Let's say that you have discovered a scrape line which begins near a thick bedding area high on a hardwood ridge. A half-dozen scrapes run along the spine of the ridge. A smattering of scrapes on small flat spots and multiple rubs, allow you to follow the scrape line down the slope, where the scraping action is heavy along a skinny creek-bottom and even more pronounced along the edge of an alfalfa field where deer are obviously feeding. The biggest scrape, a huge pawing about the size of the hood on a 1961 Caddy is located right on the edge of the alfalfa field. The temptation to doctor up that big scrape and hang a stand nearby is great. After all, any scrape that big is getting a lot of attention from more than one buck, right? That's true. Community scrapes that are routinely visited by more than one buck are fairly common and most of them, just like the one you found, are located at or near the food source. The reason for this is because the chow line is where all of the bucks and does get together each evening to feed and play out the ancient rutting ritual.

The problem with hunting a big scrape like the one you found is that nearly all visits to it are going to be made after or before shooting hours. The odds of a mature buck visiting a scrape along the edge of an open field in broad daylight aren't good. So as difficult as it is to ignore those big, stinking-fresh community scrapes, I'll usually opt for doctoring a scrape or two up on that hardwood ridge instead. My reasoning is simple. Odds

and again. If you can get a buck or bucks to make frequent visits to a favorite scrape, just as our family makes frequent visits to our favorite restaurant, the odds of a buck showing up during shooting hours escalate. Otherwise you're left sitting in that tree with the gnawing knowledge that study after study has shown 75 percent of scrape visits are made under the cover of darkness. That's not the kind of information that gives you the confidence needed to hunt a scrape line all day when the rut is peaking.

Some hunters are concerned that if they mess with a scrape, they might spook the buck. I've never seen a buck spook or shy away from a doctored scrape. I'm not saying that it never happens, because there are obviously many visits to my doctored scrapes that occur at night, and I have no idea what takes place during those nocturnal visits. But the fact that I've never seen a buck become suspicious of a scrape I've doctored tells me the odds of one spooking from a doctored scrape are slim at best. I've heard other hunters relate horror stories about bucks spooking from their doctored scrapes, but after I've questioned these individuals about the particulars, in each case I've found they are that the buck I'm after isn't going to vacate his bedding area in the evening until shortly before last light, and that the buck's going to be back in the security of his thicket by full light in the morning. My best chance of intercepting him, morning or evening, is by hunting over a scrape near his bedding area.

Another reason I prefer to doctor scrapes near the bedding area is because I routinely sit in a stand all day when the rut's in progress. A mature buck is probably not going to get out of his bed and make the trip all the way to the field edge to check out that big community scrape, but there's an excellent chance that sometime during the day he'll get antsy and wander along that ridge to freshen his nearest scrapes.

My hunting journal indicates most of these midday visits to scrapes near a bedding area take place between 11 a.m and 1:30 p.m. I don't think it's coincidental that these are also the hours when the fewest hunters are still on stand.

How many scrapes I doctor depends on several factors. In the diagram on page 38, I doctored three scrapes on the ridge, but the only reason I doctored three was that all were within range of my stand. Never doctor a scrape that's not within range of your stand. I've seen bucks spend 20 minutes at a doctored scrape, and the last thing you want to have is a buck working a doctored scrape down the line while you're sitting in your stand 100 yards away with light fading fast. You'll also notice that I've hung two stands, one on the north side of the doctored scrapes and one on the south side. This way, if the wind is from either direction I can hunt my doctored scrapes without fear of being scented by deer.

There's a third stand hung near a doctored scrape along the creek. The ridge stands are my primary stands, but the creek stand is my ace-in-the-hole in case the wind shifts to an easterly direction. An east wind would make either of the ridge stands unhuntable because the wind would be carrying my scent into the bedding area. Even though I'm as fussy and careful about controlling human odor as anyone I know, I'd never tempt fate by hunting a stand upwind of a bedding area. It's just too risky.

When To Doctor A Scrape

Anytime you find active scrapes is a good time to doctor them, but the best time in my experience is when the first scrapes start to appear. The first scrapes in the woods are almost always made by the dominant buck in an area. Because mature bucks begin scraping (and rubbing) earlier than immature bucks, this is your best chance to concentrate on a real bruiser. A week or two after the big boys lay down their scrapes, the other bucks in the area will get in on the scraping game and then it becomes more difficult to target an individual buck.

One of the best ways to get a big buck's attention is to make a couple of mock scrapes (see sidebar on page 41) in his territory before he begins to make his own scrapes. This gets the attention of a dominant buck in a hurry!

Doctoring scrapes works up until the bucks abandon their scrapes to concentrate on trailing, tending and breeding with estrous does. I've tried doctoring scrapes I've found during that brief fling known as the "second rut" when some of the

Adding a quality lure to an overhanging tree limb completes the mock scrape sham.

It's hard to argue with results like this ... the author with a trophy whitetail taken at a doctored scrape.

female fawns and any does that didn't conceive during the main rut cycle comes back into estrus, but I've found it to be a waste of effort.

HOW TO DOCTOR A SCRAPE

As long as you keep human odor out of the equation, there's no single formula for doctoring a scrape. I can tell you how I do it and what I use, and you're welcome to take my recipe and put it to work for you this fall, modify it or come up with your own method. Scrapes are all about scent communication and the most important communicator isn't the scrape itself, but rather the overhanging branch.

When a buck works an overhanging branch, he leaves scent behind from his forehead glands, pre-orbital glands, nasal glands, saliva glands and I suspect, since a buck frequently licks his tarsal glands, that scent from this gland and the urine that dribbles over the tarsal is also left behind. To my knowledge, there's no deer scent on the market that precisely matches all these odors.

Fortunately for us, deer are curious creatures and are attracted to a variety of scents.

For many years I used doe-in-estrus urine on overhanging branches over scrapes. I've never seen a doe big enough to urinate on an overhanging branch, but that didn't register with the many bucks that came in to work those doctored branches. I'd still be using doe urine on the over-hanging branch if the scent industry hadn't come up with better options.

Today, there are many scents on the market that incorporate the odors from one or more of the glands I just mentioned. Primetime Buck Lure Supreme 1, Mrs. Doe Pee's Freeze Dried Buck Tarsal and a synthetic lure called Rut from Hawg's Limited are three that I've used with good success.

I like to apply a little to the branch itself and then use a plastic tie or piece of wire to secure a scent wick to the branch. Soak the wick in scent and it'll last for a long time. If you don't wire the wick to the branch, bucks will chew it off or hook it off with their antlers.

When doctoring scrapes I like to take a stout

stick, put some gel or paste lure such as James Valley Wallhanger on the end of the stick and use it to work up the dirt in the scrape while adding the scent right to the dirt. Then I pour in about a cup of Magic Scrape, which is a waterproof soil that holds scents for a long time.

In the mound of Magic Scrape, I make a small indentation and add about a half-ounce of a liquid lure. Primetime Whitetail Fresh Scrape is a blend of doe-in-estrus urine, buck urine and tarsal gland secretions that I've used with good success. I've also had good luck with straight buck urine such as Mrs. Doe Pee's Buck-In-Rut and doe-in-estrus urine from a number of scent companies.

A doctored scrape, like many of the other tricks whitetail hunters use, is no cure-all. I've had bucks ignore my doctored scrapes many times. But I've also had them come to doctored scrapes on enough occasions that there's no doubt in my mind that a little doctoring is a healthy habit to get into when it comes to targeting big bucks.

Making the Most of Mock Scrapes

Mock scrapes are most effective if you make them before bucks begin pawing out their own scrapes. When a buck discovers a mock scrape prior to the time he's begun scraping, it invokes both curiosity and aggression—a double-whammy that's likely to keep him visiting your mock scrape in an attempt to find the buck that made it. If you wait until bucks are scraping on their own, your mock scrape will compete with natural scrapes and draw less interest from bucks.

As in a real scrape, the most important part of a mock scrape is the overhanging branch. Choose a branch about 5 feet off the ground. If a suitable branch isn't available at the location where you'd like to make a mock scrape, cut a branch from another tree and wire it into position. Doctor the overhanging branch just as you would the overhanging branch at a real scrape.

To make the scrape I use a garden trowel to clear a spot on the ground about the size of a beach ball. With the trowel I work up the soil while at the same time working in some scent and burying that scent about an inch under the soil. This trick will keep bucks coming back and you can do it several ways. One is to poke holes in the top of a small jar (baby food jars are perfect), add the scent of your choice and bury the jar so that the lid is about an inch under the dirt. You can do the same with a 35mm film canister by stuffing the canister with clean cotton and saturating the cotton with your favorite liquid scent, paste or gel lure. Another option is to bury an H.S. Scents BucRut wafer—these plastic, scent-impregnated wafers give off odor for a week or more and will keep bucks coming to your mock scrape between hunts.—*Gary Clancy*

PART II

Hunt
Them

Whitetail hunting is not for the lazy of body or the meek of heart, for you will not find a more challenging big game animal on Earth. But that doesn't mean that you need the fanciest equipment, the most of it, or even a complicated game plan, to be successful in whitetail country. In fact, the best hunters take the simplest approaches. But what sets these whitetail fanatics apart is their dedication ... a true zest for deer hunting and an unwavering commitment to working hard, all day, every grand day they get to spend on their whitetail quest.

BUCK BLUNDERS

Avoid these common mistakes and bring home your buck.

BY GARY CLANCY

*I*f you were to ever visit my home, you might—or might not—be impressed by the number and size of the white-tailed deer mounts that clutter my office. It wouldn't matter to me what you thought of them, or if you were to even notice them, because I had the bucks mounted for me—and for them. When I look at the mounts, I remember how each deer looked before I pulled the trigger or dropped the bowstring. I recall the way the woods looked and smelled, the way my heart pounded and how my right leg got to jumping. I mounted each of those deer as a tribute to them, because to my way of thinking, a mature buck deserves nothing less.

The deer on my walls have all been my teachers, and I've learned something from each of them. But the most valuable lessons I've learned in the way of the whitetail have been taught by bucks that never got to make that final ride in the bed of my pickup truck. It's the ones I've botched that have taught me the most.

I'd like you to believe I made all eight of the following buck blunders many years ago, and that after four decades of hunting deer I've got it all figured out. But that's not the case.

NO. 1: NOT LISTENING TO FARMERS.
Last fall, I'd drawn an Iowa archery tag and was hunting on two farms owned by friends in the central part of the state. The farms were a few miles apart and I'd often hunt one of them in the morning and the other during the afternoon.

Several times during the first week I hunted the farms, one of the farm hands mentioned to me they'd seen a good buck behind the house on the property. Nobody lived in the house, but the farmer kept cattle on the farm, so twice a day one of the workers or the owner would show up to do chores. Since my buddy Matt and I already had five stands hung where we figured were the best places on the farm, I didn't pay much attention to the farm hand. Besides, the corner of the woods where he'd been seeing the buck was only about 75 yards behind the house, so I ignored the tip. Then one afternoon as I walked to my stand, I happened to spot a nice buck in that corner of woods behind the house. He was standing there, watching me. I kept walking, knowing if I stopped and put my binoculars on him, he'd know I'd seen him, which might make him spook. I made a

Farmers have access to their land 24 hours a day. If they give you a tip on a good buck, take it seriously.

Seeing a buck once doesn't constitute a pattern. Watch the area for a couple days and then decide on a course of action.

use it. I'd missed out, and it was all because I hadn't listened to the farm hand.

No. 2: Sounding An Alarm.

I had a .50-caliber Thompson/Center Hawken sitting on my lap. I was new to muzzleloading, having taken my first muzzleloader deer with the same rifle the previous year. It had snowed 6 inches during the night, soft snow that not only made the woods beautiful, but quiet as well. That's how one buck got within 60 yards of me before I saw him. Head down and nose to the ground, he was cruising for does, oblivious to the fact that death sat perched in the spreading branches of a maple on the side of the ridge. When a deer's that close and closing fast, you tend to panic a bit, or at least I did. Without thinking I thumbed back the big hammer on the Hawken. It locked into place with a metallic click so loud in that silent, white cathedral that the buck skidded to a halt, looked right at me, turned and ran, all at a rate quicker than you can read this sentence.

That evening, sitting in an easy chair in my living room, I kept the Hawken, now unloaded, sprawled across my lap. Every few minutes I'd reach down, apply pressure to the trigger and thumb back the hammer. Once the hammer was all the way back I'd release the pressure on the trigger. It's a silent method of engaging the hammer that's served me well ever since.

mental note to check that corner out the next day, but I never got around to it.

It was a week later when I finally snooped around that unlikely corner of timber behind the house. What I found nearly made me sick to my stomach: Every small tree in the corner had been savagely rubbed raw, and huge scrapes littered the ground. It was obvious I was looking at a major staging area, one used by multiple bucks. But what hurt the most was I knew it was too late to take advantage of the gold mine because the rut was on the downhill slide. A staging area like this one

Learning how to silently engage your firearm could be well worth the effort.

is used during pre-rut and the early stages of the rut. Once the does come into heat, bucks that had been using the staging area on a regular basis switch their attention to the does and no longer

No. 3: Setting Up Too Soon.

You read and hear a lot about patterning deer, but it's not as easy as some make it out to be. The problem is, depending on the time of year, deer are just not all that dependable in their habits. For many years, I made the mistake of seeing a buck once and then setting up on him after that one sighting. Rarely did the buck show up again near my stand. Then about 15 years ago, I wrote an article about Myles Keller, a Minnesota bowhunter with an uncanny ability to put good bucks on the ground. When I interviewed Myles for that article, there was one thing he said that hit me like a hammer: "If I see a buck once in an area, I'll watch the place for another day or two," he said. "If I see that buck at about the same time again, I'll go in and hang my stand. Most of the time I'll kill that buck. But if I don't see the buck again, I start looking for him or his sign somewhere else. Seeing a buck once is a start, but it's not reason enough for me to hang a stand there."

NO. 4: FOCUSING ON ANTLERS.

Many years ago, when I was brand-new to bowhunting, I had an encounter with a real bruiser. Hunters in the area called him "Old Patches" because of a couple of white patches of hair on his flank. Like every other hunter, I dreamed of someday getting a shot at "Old Patches" and by golly, one day I did. It was an easy shot, too, well within range of my recurve. But I blew it because I couldn't take my eyes off his rack. And when I released that cedar arrow it went right where I was looking. The arrow rattled around harmlessly in the buck's mass of twisted bone and then fell to the ground. That was during the 1960s, and to this day, when I have a good buck approaching, I begin my chant: "Don't look at the antlers. Don't look at the antlers. Don't look at the … ."

NO. 5: NOT PRACTICING IN YOUR HUNTING CLOTHES.

Like you, I've read a thousand times that you should practice shooting before the season with what you'll be wearing in your stand. This is especially true for bowhunters. Sometimes I heed that advice, but like you, sometimes I get in a hurry and don't. And that cost me a big deer a couple years back. Scent-Lok had come out with a new hood and despite my best intentions to do so, I

Practice in the clothing you'll wear into your stand to identify and eliminate any potential problems, snags or catches.

never did get out and practice shooting while actually wearing it. Then, during the opening evening of the bow season in my home state of Minnesota, I had a dandy buck make his way slowly down the trail in front of me. Everything was perfect. The light was good, the buck was at ease and my shooting lane, which had been cleared nearly two months prior to the season, was old news to the big buck. Just before he stepped into my shooting lane I drew and grunted softly. The buck stopped in mid-stride right in the middle of that shooting lane. He even had his near foreleg forward. Everything was textbook, except for one minor detail: When I drew my bow, my thumb hooked the drawstring of my new hood, which in turn, tugged the fabric of the hood down and to the right. I was blinded. By

Shoot! Take the first good shot a buck gives you. You might not get another one.

tilting my head up I could see the buck standing there, but there was no way I could see my pins. While I panicked, the buck flicked his tail and calmly walked off.

After he was gone, I tightened up the drawstring, adjusted it to ride higher on my head and drew again with no problem. If I'd made that minor adjustment a month before the season when I should have, my biggest Minnesota buck to date would now be hanging on my wall.

No. 6: Passing Up The First Good Shot.

The long-necked doe was obviously in estrus and the buck on her tail knew it. He dogged her every step. As they worked up the ridge toward where I was perched in a gnarly, old oak, I put the glasses on the buck and instantly knew the tall-tined 10-pointer would easily make the "Clancy Book," which is the only one that really matters to me. There were two options for a shot. One was 26 yards from the base of my tree, and the other was seven steps closer. As the doe stepped into the first opening I drew my bow and waited for the buck to step in behind her. He did, but for some reason I decided to wait for them to cross into the second shooting lane. But they never made it. In the 20 or

so feet separating the two shooting lanes, a scrubby little 7-pointer with big ideas came bounding over the ridge and made a beeline for the doe. She took off with the 7-pointer on her tail and the big buck lumbering along after both of them.

Another time I had a nice 8-pointer come to my decoy. The buck stopped at about 25 yards and offered me a good quartering-away shot as he stared at the decoy. I thought about taking the shot, but didn't. Instead, I waited for the buck to fully commit to the decoy and present me with one of those slam-dunk 15-yard broadside shots that are the rule when hunting over a buck decoy. But this buck didn't like something he saw. Or maybe he just wasn't in the mood for a fight, because he turned and walked away. I grunted at him, but he never even stopped to look back.

Today, whether I'm hunting with gun or bow, I take the first good shot offered. Most of the time, that's been the right decision.

No. 7: Leaving For Lunch.

Anytime the rut is in progress, try to stay in your stand from 10 a.m. until at least 2 p.m. Sitting all day is even better, but if you can't hack it on stand all day, be sure to spend this four-hour stretch in one of your best spots. I can't begin to count the number of good bucks I've seen on the prowl between 10 and 2.

There was a time, however, when I didn't heed my own advice. Twice in the same week, I climbed down from my stand at midday and spooked off good bucks within 100 yards of my location. Either of those two might have offered me a shot if I'd just stayed put. From then on, whenever I want to abandon ship at midday, I remember the sight of those two monsters. It helps me stay put.

Another part of the year when you'll want to stay in the woods during late morning and early afternoon is during the firearms deer season, especially opening weekend. With all the other hunters coming and going, attempting to still-hunt and put on drives, you never know when a buck is going to get bumped and come sneaking past your stand. I've killed a bunch of good deer while other hunters were back at camp having lunch or taking a nap.

NO. 8: FEAR OF MAKING NOISE.

Like many of you, I was taught to sit still and be quiet when deer hunting. That made it hard for me to purposefully make noise by blowing on a grunt call or rattling antlers. But after 15 years of serious rattling and calling, I know now I've missed out on some great action by not making some noise in the woods earlier in my deer hunting career.

One of the most painful lessons I've learned involved an absolute giant of a non-typical and a set of rattling antlers. It was mid-November in western Illinois, and I'd been rattling off and on for three days, but so far had managed to attract only two small bucks. During the fourth day, I hadn't see a deer by late morning, so for the umpteenth time, I grabbed the rattling antlers from the branch stub on which they hung and started a short rattling sequence. It's my habit to hang the antlers back up and grab my bow or gun after every sequence, because I know how fast a buck can appear. If you wait until a buck is in sight before you try to hang up the antlers and get your hands on your bow or gun, there's a good chance the buck will spot you. But I got lazy this time. And I suppose after four days of not having much action, I wasn't feeling too confident about anything responding to the rattling. So like a dummy, I stood there in my treestand with those antlers in my hands. The buck came in behind me, from straight downwind. I'm a nut about odor control and on this morning I was wearing two Scent-Lok suits, which is probably the only reason the buck didn't smell me. The wind was making enough noise that I didn't hear the buck coming either. When I finally heard something and turned around to look, he was standing a dozen steps behind my tree. If I would've had a buck decoy out in front of me, the buck probably would've walked right in, but I didn't. He wanted to see the

deer he'd heard fighting, so he stood for a minute or two, checking the wind some, but mostly just looking for that other deer. I knew he was going to lose interest and walk away, so as slowly as I could, I reached up and hooked my rattling antlers on a branch stub. I got away with it, too, but when I took my hands off the antlers to reach for my bow, the two antlers made contact. It was just a little click, but it was enough to make the buck look up at me. Already nervous, he turned and hurried off.

Ever since, no matter how tired I am, or how little confidence I have that a buck might actually show, I hang those antlers up and get my bow or gun in hand during each pause in my rattling sequence.

After 40 years of deer hunting, these are some of the blunders I've made and the lessons I've learned. Lessons taught to me by the best teachers in the whitetail woods. And even after all these years, I know the deer still have more to teach me.

Don't be afraid to make something happen in the woods. Just remember to put down the antlers and pick up your gun or bow.

THE WONDERS OF WATER

Whitetails require water. Pinpointing these areas might bring you the buck of a lifetime.

By Scott Bestul

Some maps lead you to treasure, others send you on snipe hunts. I didn't know what to make of the one in my hand. Scratched on a piece of paper two hours earlier by my buddy Don, the map led me across 10 miles of Kansas prairie to a spot I'd have driven past any other day. Don is a rancher, not a deer hunter, but when he handed me the map he'd issued a work order: "There are two big bucks hanging out here," he said, jabbing his finger into the pencil lines. "Go shoot one."

I've seen my share of whitetail cover, and this was slim pickings, even for western Kansas. Scattered cottonwoods, some prairie brush, a handful of cedars … at first glance, the kind of place that would get a pheasant hunter—not someone after a mature buck—excited. But as I readied for a quick scouting session, I noted harvested corn and milo fields nearby, as well as two decent CRP tracts. "OK," I thought, trying to talk myself into things, "they've got food and a little bedding cover. Is that enough for a tiny place like this?"

I got my answer less than 100 yards from the truck. I practically stumbled into a creek, a clear-water rill I could have hopped across. But deer tracks peppered its banks and deep-gouged crossings looked like they'd been cut by cattle hooves. Five minutes later, I bumped a bedded buck that was surely one of the deer Don had spotted. I hunted that little creek-bottom in the middle of nowhere for the next three days and was slack-jawed at the number of whitetails it held. I was within bow range of a monster buck on three different occasions and, although luck saved his hide

each time, I count that hunt among my most memorable.

I'm convinced water is what made that little patch of prairie shine. Like most hunters, I've devoted endless time and energy to finding food, cover and buck sign through the years, but water was barely on my radar. As I've discovered on deer hunts across the country, however, water is a huge draw for whitetails. And any time I've been fortunate to find a key water source, I've experienced good hunting.

BASIC NEEDS?

I grew up believing whitetails weren't big on drinking and got most of the H_2O they needed from the plants they consumed. As a kid I read articles about the subject and accepted it as Gospel, because one of my early goals (before I was old enough to hunt) was to actually see a deer drinking. I was so wet behind the ears that when I finally spotted a young buck sipping from a stream, I figured I'd witnessed a Marlon Perkins moment! Things didn't improve much when I started hunting. I cut my deer hunting teeth in central Wisconsin, where you can't walk a quarter-mile without encountering a lake, creek or swamp. Since deer there don't have to work hard to find water, I almost ignored water unless I was crossing a stream to get to one of my stands.

Though deer certainly obtain moisture from feed—especially during summer—they'll drink heartily (and often) if water is available. And in

When the rut is in full swing, a water source will commonly be a hotbed of whitetail activity.

many instances, such as extended periods of heat or drought, water becomes critical to deer and they'll go out of their way to find it.

But you don't have to visit the desert to find thirsty deer. Once the chasing phase of the rut begins, whitetails get very serious about drinking. It took my friend Ted Marum, owner of Buffalo County Outfitters, to teach me about the importance of re-hydrating to rutting whitetails. "Think about it," Ted explained to me. "You're wearing a fur coat that can keep you warm in sub-zero temps. You're running after does for hours every day. If you don't drink water, you're gonna tip over. It doesn't matter where bucks live; once the rut kicks in, they're gonna look for water." Consequently, Ted has focused much of his energy hunting near water sources, and the success rates of his hunters have risen exponentially since he made that decision.

Drinking isn't the only reason whitetails gravitate to water sources. Many of their favorite browse and plant species grow along water courses, making a stream bank or lakeshore the equivalent of a salad bar. Even better, plants growing near a wetland are typically the first to green up and the last to die off, so deer searching for moisture-rich foods come fall will likely wind up near water. And it's no secret that wet areas are often surrounded by dense brush and trees that whitetails prefer for bedding. When I look back at the dozens of deer drives my cousins and I made during the high-pressure circus of the Wisconsin firearms season, I remember our most successful pushes occurred in the thick growth along the

creeks, lakes and swamps on our property.

Finally, and of no less importance, water sources serve as natural travel corridors for deer. Whitetails—especially big-running bucks—have a very simple criteria when they move from Point A to Point B: They want the easiest, fastest route, and they want cover that hides them as they move. River systems meet those requirements perfectly. If you doubt this, visit an unfamiliar property (or even one you've hunted for years) and walk along a river bank or stream course. In addition to the dozens of crossings you'll find, there'll be at least one heavy trail paralleling the water; an easy, secluded thoroughfare for whitetails.

GETTING YOUR FEET WET

Naturally, not all water sources are created equally. Tagging a buck near any micro-habitat involves knowing when he's most likely to visit the area, and that includes both the time of year and day.

That whitetails are cover-oriented, light-shy critters is one of the first lessons of Deer Hunting 101. These traits mean you can rule out most water sources in open areas. I hunt a farm with a nice, spring-fed pond that sits at the intersection of a pasture and a cultivated field. Those pond

Besides being prime areas for their favorite browse, creeks can also provide high-quality cover and convenient travel routes for whitetails.

Two effective methods of creating artificial water sources on a property include using machinery to create "push-up" ponds (left), or by hand-digging a hole for a landscaping pond (right).

banks are positively littered with deer tracks, including some obvious buck prints. But, most of those deer aren't reaching that water until the last shred of light during hunting season. I've found this situation holds largely true regardless of region. Unless you're hunting a prairie area and your pond offers the only drink for miles, don't count on deer hitting it until well after nightfall.

Conversely, water sources surrounded by woods or those situated close to other security cover will be visited by deer throughout the day, especially when the weather is warm or during the rut. Marum has gone out of his way to discover, and set his hunters near, such protected water sources. "Once I started doing that, our opportunities on mature bucks skyrocketed," Marum said. "If I can find a pond or other water source near a bedding area, I know I've got a hotspot that will produce the entire fall if I hunt it right."

Ted is so sold on this tactic he'll create small "push-up" ponds on properties. Once he's located a prime location (usually a wooded ridgetop where he can count on consistent wind directions), he hires a CAT operator to dig out a 10-square-feet knee- to waist-deep waterhole. "We dig until we hit clay, so that way we know the pond will hold water," Marum said. "And then we just let the rain fill them up. If you have sandy or rocky soil, you might want to add a liner."

If you want to create a pond but can't afford a dozer, there's a cheaper route. Buy a landscaping pond or hard-rubber livestock tank, dig a hole big enough to set the tub in and backfill around it. I have another hunting buddy who's done this in several locations on his farm and has seen impressive results. "I felt a little silly on the first one I put in," my friend admitted. "But on the opening day of archery season I watched six different bucks come into that tub!"

The key in any such setup is to pick your treestand or blind location first, then dig the pond. And before you hunt it, determine a silent entry path that will allow you access without spooking bedded deer. Discipline yourself to only hunt there when the wind is correct, and you should have a hotspot that will produce until the water freezes over.

If I had my druthers, however, I'd pick smaller water sources over large ones. My experience has been that smaller bodies of water tend to focus deer activity, a situation that is both a blessing and a curse. The blessing comes in the form of concentrated deer sign and more obvious setups; a huge deal if I'm on an out-of-state hunt and have only a few days of opportunity. The curse occurs when you realize these micro-habitats require much more careful hunting. If a big buck doesn't show up in the first sit or two, alerting other deer and "polluting" the spot is a real concern.

While I haven't given up on nailing down the richest feed, the hottest buck sign and the thoroughfare trails I've always searched for, I now concentrate most heavily on the very thing I used to ignore. Water is hot stuff!

Hunting the Deer Farm

Follow these strategies for consistent success on farmland deer.

By Tom Carpenter

White-tailed deer survive and adapt magnificently, and they've made themselves right at home in the nation's farmlands. Food is everywhere and when you add cover in the form of woodlots, creek- or river-bottoms, wetlands and maybe a few fallow fields, you've got deer heaven.

That abundance of deer—including some very big bucks—makes up for any lack of wilderness in the hunting experience. Yet I find it hard to imagine a scene prettier than a patchwork of autumn woods, cut cornfields, plowed ground, still-green hay fields and tawny meadows—punctuated by barns and silos here and there—rolling off the horizon.

Regardless of where you hunt farmland whitetail, success starts with understanding the following deer behaviors:

- **COOL UNDER PRESSURE.** Farmland deer don't panic under hunting pressure. They'll sit incredibly tight and let danger pass, often within spitting distance or less. Or they'll use their eyes, ears and nose to identify problems before they happen, then sneak out ahead of any approaching danger.
- **NOT AFRAID OF OPEN COUNTRY.** When it's time to move—or make an escape—farmland deer do it now, and usually on a straight line from point A to point B. They have no reservations about crossing open country. In fact, I think they sometimes prefer the visibility that open fields afford.
- **MASTERS OF HIDING.** Farmland whitetails often evade hunters by practicing patience and nerves instead of hoofbeats and surprise. And don't

believe that deer are always hiding in "classic" (read: forest) cover. In fact, farmland whitetails often prefer areas that are meager in cover but rich in seclusion.

- **HOMEBODIES.** It's almost impossible to chase a farmland deer out of its home range. Sure, you might rout an animal out, but it will return ... often during daylight. When deer seem scarce, it's easy to believe they have vacated the premises or vanished entirely. But they're most likely right there next to you, hiding in the places they know best.

SIMPLE STRATEGIES

The two best strategies for killing farmland deer are simple: have the right attitude and spend plenty of time in the field.

By a deer farm's very nature (open fields, abundant deer, lots of edge cover, other hunters shunting whitetails about), it can produce hunting action quickly and unexpectedly. You have to be out there and ready.

Consider my "10 seconds to success" rule. Pick any one moment in time, and you can have a deer down in 10 seconds ... but only if you're out hunting, and only if you're ready and in the right frame of mind at all times.

Should you head in for lunch? No way. Mornings and evenings are fine, but farmland whitetails will move during midday to get back into their core ranges or to feed for a few moments. Other hunters will move deer about the countryside, too. So be out there hunting.

No Trees Needed

Trees aren't essential for good whitetail cover, but hunters seemingly always head to wooded places. And when they do, the deer often go somewhere else.

My friend Reynold's farm has 10 acres of woods on 200 acres of land. But we find deer in a brushy old railroad right-of-way, a wet pasture that's abandoned to marsh, a cattail marsh and the brushy banks of the creek that bisects the farm. CRP land and fallow fields also make great deer hideouts.—*Tom Carpenter*

Put in your time during the course of a season. Maybe everything's not going your way today, but tomorrow or the next day could be better. Sooner or later, success will find you.

HUNTING PLANS

Stand hunting and farmland deer go hand-in-hand. The best way to find good stand sites is to hunt an area for a season or two and see the deer in action—find out where they travel naturally, and where they travel (and hole up) under pressure.

On one farm I hunt, there are stand sites that have produced deer for more than a quarter-century! On the other hand, land-use changes can turn a hotspot into a dud—and back again—year by year. Crop rotation, logging activity, a new house being built somewhere … they can all change your hunting, and sometimes for the better. Stick with proven areas until you have compelling reasons to move, but don't be afraid to make that change.

Farmland is open country, and many stand sites overlook fields. Likely spots include a corner where a fencerow or other cover meets a woodlot, a point of woods or finger of brush jutting into a field, a four-way fence corner and a T-shaped fence corner.

Deer farm whitetails have a way of using terrain to make themselves disappear, so get to know the dips and folds of the land around your stand sites. Conversely, deer can pop up seemingly out of thin air when they use terrain for cover as they move.

When hunting fieldside, back up to a tree, fencepost or other edge cover to break up your silhouette. Get a little elevation if you can and hunt with intensity and purpose, minimizing movement. You never know from which direction a deer will come, so take a thorough scan before wiping your nose, reaching for a cup of coffee, etc.

I'm not a big fan of treestands on field edges, because by gun season, with all the leaves down, you're extra visible to deer already wary of perched bowhunters. And November and December's bitter winds can be tough on a person.

Another good stand strategy is to wait in the places where deer go to escape hunting pressure. You won't see as many deer in these locations, simply because you'll be in thick cover. But if you wait long enough, you'll kill a deer.

If stand hunting isn't productive, team up with one or two hunting partners and do some little "pushes." These hunts aren't deer drives, because

Find a likely ambush point where deer want to go and be prepared to stay there all day.

farmland whitetails go where they want to. All you can do is get them up and moving and hope they go toward your well-positioned posters. If you know the land and the deer, and plan right, it works.

Pick small pieces of cover to push. A couple hundred yards' worth of cover is enough; less is better. The farther you try to move a farmland whitetail, the more alternate escape routes it has at its disposal.

Get posters into position without the deer seeing or smelling them, and place them along escape routes, or in cover the deer might head to. Putting posters near the cover you're going to push will just alert the whitetails, and they'll sneak out early or not move at all.

Get in the cover and push deer with a purpose. Whitetails will stay right where they are, safe and sound, if the pusher is out for an easy autumn stroll.

Always follow these basic safety rules: Posters should never shoot in the direction from which pushers are coming, and should let the deer pass into safe shooting lanes. Pushers can shoot, but never in the direction of any posters or other pushers. And posters should stay put until the pushers are completely done and at their side. Action can—and often does—erupt late in any push, and it's safer to have everybody where they're supposed to be.

GOOD HUNTING, GOOD PLACE

"Deer season!" These two words evoke images of a rustic cabin or traditional tent camp, big woods far from civilization and wilderness deer. I like that experience and still get a fix from it every year.

But the deer season that really gets my blood pumping happens out there amongst a rolling rural patchwork of woodlots and forgotten corners gone wild. It's here, in this mosaic of edges in which whitetails thrive, that I return every year for a deer hunting rite that's integral to my life.

I find great satisfaction just being on the deer farms of autumn. And it doesn't hurt that the deer love these places, too ... providing opportunities to fill my gunsights with a fat whitetail, my freezer with venison and my heart with the best kind of memories.

Barnyard Buck

The old pasture behind my friend Walter's barn had been without cows for about a decade—long enough to become overgrown with raspberry brambles and other assorted brush amongst a few old white oaks. It was a great whitetail hideout and would make a great place to wait for a deer.

I greeted my friends as usual that opening morning, and even had a cup of coffee in the kitchen because I didn't have far to go to get to my stand. Before shooting light I was positioned next to one of those giant oaks.

At 6:45 a.m., I heard hoofbeats—not the pitter-patter of deer, but Herefords clumping up to the barn for their morning grain. At 7 a.m., a tractor started up—Saturday morning barnyard cleaning.

At 7:15 a.m., I discerned the telltale thump of deer hooves over frozen ground. A buck hopped the fence, entering my gully from a hilltop alfalfa field.

I slowly brought my slug gun up, leaned against the furrowed bark of the steady oak and pulled the trigger.

The buck folded at my shot. I walked over and sat beside the young 5-pointer for a few minutes, feeling every bit like I was a great buckskin-clad deerslayer in the great wilderness ... except for the white barn I could see through the trees and the combine now combing the river-bottom cornfields.—*Tom Carpenter*

BACKYARD BUCKS

You don't have to go to the wilderness to shoot big bucks.

BY TODD AMENRUD

What a terrible afternoon of hunting! Two riders had been by on horseback along the neighbor's property line, and the other neighbor's son was now on his ATV tearing up the ground. He was buzzing so close to my treestand I had to turn my face because the breeze was carrying the dust right toward me. Disappointed, I was about ready to get out of my stand when I spotted a flicker of antler in the sunlight. Through my binoculars I saw a big buck bedded only 100 yards away. Now I couldn't move, nor did I want to!

The afternoon went on and I continued to curse the ATV rider. "If it weren't for that 'bleeping' four-wheeler I'd have my trophy. That kid has screwed up everything for me." It was amazing: The buck was bedded within 30 yards of the ATV trail, but the noise didn't seem to bother him a bit. Finally, the sun started dropping behind the trees and the neighbor kid went home. After only a minute or two, a doe popped up out of her nearby bed and ambled by my stand. Even though the leaves were dry, I could hardly hear her because the rush hour traffic on the nearby highway sounded like flies buzzing in my ears.

My binoculars stayed glued on the buck. At long last he stood and stretched. He waved his nose in the air to scent-check the area and then started browsing in my direction. When he reached 22 yards, I sent a broadhead through his lungs, and he expired less than 100 yards away.

Suburban bucks, such as this big 7x7 arrowed by the author, have an excellent chance to reach full maturity because gun seasons are typically closed in these areas.

Scouting too much during the season for fresh rubs or other sign can actually hurt your chances for success because mature bucks quickly learn they're being hunted.

CLOSE TO HOME

During the first cool days of late summer, hunters begin talking to their buddies about the upcoming deer season—going to "deer camp." What many of these individuals don't know is some of the best deer hunting available is right in their own backyard.

Whitetails have flourished in many suburban areas throughout North America. In fact, human development of land, which has created a high-percentage of edge cover, has been a blessing for whitetails. Let me give you a real-life example.

I grew up on a property that three years ago turned into a "century farm." My family has owned this farm in Minnesota for more than 100 years, and during the past couple decades I've seen this area change from mature forest with a few dirt roads to a Minneapolis suburb. Today, much of the area around the farm contains housing developments, baseball and soccer fields and a network of paved roads. My worst fear while living here has been that my hunting spots would all be developed and eaten up by the urban sprawl. While that has somewhat come to pass, what I've found is the hunting has actually gotten better,

especially for mature bucks. With the houses spaced so close together, many places that used to be open for gun hunting are now open only for archery hunting—obviously bad for a gun hunter, but great for a bowhunter. This factor now gives bucks a great chance to live past 1 ½ years of age, and with age comes a chance to sport some decent head gear.

There's no question I've had to change with the times. I used to go to my neighbor's house, knock on their door and ask permission to bowhunt their property. They'd laugh at me and say, "Bowhunt? Have at it. You actually hunt with a bow?" Now, however, it's especially difficult to gain access close to large metro areas, mainly because there are so many more people fighting for such a smaller piece of the pie.

With a little persistence and digging, however, accessing these metro hotspots can be done. In fact, one can also explore the public hunting opportunities close to large metro areas or look into organizations such as Minnesota's Metro Bowhunters Resource Base (MBRB).

In response to the unchecked growth of white-tail populations in urban environments, representatives from Minnesota's leading archery organizations joined forces in 1995 to form the MBRB. The group works with the Minnesota Department of Natural Resources and metro communities to generate bowhunting opportunities. It assists these communities when needed in the planning and administering of special bowhunts. And here's the best part: It also supplies competent and responsible bowhunters for the programs. Other large metro areas across the country also have organizations such as this, and you can learn about them by asking your state game and fish department.

SCOUT SMART

In my opinion, scouting is the most important aspect leading to a successful hunt, and it's especially important for tagging metro bucks. But too many hunters "over scout" a spot and actually hurt their chances of success. If you trample through your area during the hunting season to find a fresh buck rub that might have appeared since you

Scent Strategies

Do commercial deer scents (lures) work on both suburban and wilderness whitetails? Absolutely, and not just on immature bucks and does, either. Mature bucks can be fooled, but you need to use the right type of scent in the right way.

The time of year plays a crucial role as to whether a deer scent will be effective. For example, you shouldn't use doe-in-heat scent—which accounts for more than 90 percent of all scent sold in North America—two months before the actual breeding period. Not only are bucks more focused on feeding than breeding during this time, but the scent's presence might actually alarm them.

If you want to purchase a single scent bottle to use regardless of the time of year, choose one such as Wildlife Research Center's Trail's End #307. While the manufacturer won't divulge its secret recipe, I've found it plays on a deer's natural curiosity, and I've never had it alarm deer. As the breeding season nears and bucks begin searching for an estrous doe, I switch to the company's Special Golden Estrus.

When using #307, I hang a scent-soaked wick crosswind from my stand location to lure deer from downwind. I place the wick at my maximum shooting range because I don't want a buck to catch my odor at the same time he's checking out the deer lure. Several seasons ago I arrowed a big 7x7 buck that actually had his nose touching a wick soaked in #307. This tactic is also a great way to stop a walking deer for an easier shot.

When using Golden Estrus, I lay a scent trail with the help of Wildlife Research's Pro-Drag. This durable wick comes affixed to a string that I attach to a stick. This enables me to drag a scent trail off the exact path I'm walking and leave the cleanest scent trail possible. Obviously, in thick brush I can't drag the wick off to the side, but wherever possible I believe it's best.

The author often relies on deer scent to lure bucks within shooting range. Use a Zip-loc bag to avoid touching the scent wick.

Another advantage to this type of drag is it's much easier to control through wet areas, over fences and through tall weeds. Once I've dragged the wick to my hunting location, I hang it crosswind from my stand. Any deer that follows the trail will stop in perfect position for a shot when it hits the wick.—*Todd Amenrud*

Backyard bowhunting is a great way to expand your hunting opportunities, and you'll also help the local community control its deer population. The surroundings might not be pristine … but the whitetails are there!

scouted two days ago, you're scouting too much.

Whitetails are basically "homebodies" and choose their living quarters wisely. If you intrude once, it might not be a problem. Intrude twice, however, and it's probably no problem with the does, fawns and younger bucks, but now the mature buck you've been targeting is very aware of what's going on. If you intrude a third time, the mature buck is likely going to change his address to avoid making contact with you.

Yes, metro whitetails deal with everyday disturbances like dogs and hikers, but I believe they know when they're being hunted. After all, in these areas, humans are their only predator.

My favorite time to go through an area with a fine-tooth scouting comb is March through May. During the summer and early fall, I still do a lot of scouting, but I do so from a distance with binoculars. Most evenings during the late summer you'll

find me in my truck with my two young daughters scouring the countryside for big bucks. They love to go "lookin' for deer" with Daddy. On several occasions I've learned exactly how to set up on a specific buck from long-range glassing sessions in my truck.

When the hunting season gets under way, it's important to keep on top of what's happening in terms of deer movement patterns, but be careful not to alert deer to your presence. Thankfully, this has gotten much easier in recent years thanks to affordable trail cameras. Used correctly, scouting cameras can teach you a ton about your local deer herd without disturbing them. If you think you know what's happening 24/7 in your hunting area because you hunt it two evenings a week, I'm sorry to say you don't have a clue. Scouting cameras have opened my eyes to the movement patterns of deer on my land, and they'll do the same for you.

Do Not Disturb!

While it won't take you much time to walk through a 10- to 40-acre parcel, and funnels will be blatantly obvious, these tiny tracts are difficult to hunt without spooking deer. And because these deer live in such close proximity to humans every day of the year, they know how to hide in the smallest chunks of thick cover.

Just as you should when hunting large timber or farmland, do everything you can to obtain an aerial photo or topographical map of the property. Search out several different routes to approach each stand site so you can have alternates depending upon the wind. It's especially important to remain undetected as you enter and leave a stand. If you're busted in big timber, you can usually find another good spot and still hunt the same deer. In smaller tracts, however, once you're busted, many times the game is over, particularly if you're after a specific mature buck.

While hunting these small parcels, you might be forced into setting up very close to deer bedding areas. Not only should you map out several routes to and from your stand, but go a step further and clean these trails so you can approach silently. It's a good idea to go out a month or so before the archery opener and cut silent walking trails with a pruner or weed-whacker. And after the leaves have fallen, I use a rake to remove the debris from my access trails. Because of this effort, I often see deer bedded close to me after I approach a site and climb into my treestand.

Once you have a good idea of where to set up an ambush, it's important to get your treestand or blind in place as soon as possible—before the season is best. That way, deer have time to grow accustomed to it and to go back about their business after the disturbance. Funnels created by housing subdivisions and other man-made developments often make certain stand sites productive year after year, but make sure not to over-hunt these spots. Strike only when the odds are in your favor.

It's a good idea to have several stands set up in the same ambush spot so you can hunt during different wind conditions. This also allows you to alternate stands and keep the deer guessing. I have one 30-acre chunk I hunt within 30 minutes of downtown Minneapolis where I have eight treestands set up. Some are within bow range of one another, and this way I keep things fresh and always have a spot I can hunt regardless of the wind direction.

Timing Is Everything

Like deer hunting everywhere, I believe the best time to target metro bucks is when they're chasing every doe in sight in hopes of finding one in estrus. However, there are some great hunting periods specifically related to these urban areas that might surprise you.

The land I hunt near my home is located on the boundary between gun hunting and no gun hunting, but bowhunting is permitted in the no-gun zone. You wouldn't believe the stampede of deer that come running from the gun hunting side on opening day of firearms season. Bowhunters "in the know" would never miss the chance to be set up on a funnel near that boundary when the slug gun hunters take to the woods.

Key food sources can also be obvious in metro areas where there's an absence of agricultural land. Places like apple orchards or even gardens can act as deer magnets. I like to plant food plots, and because my plots are the only major food source for some distance around, the later it gets in the season the more deer I see.

Backyard bowhunting certainly isn't for everybody. Instead of hearing wolves howling at dark, you'll hear dogs barking; and instead of seeing miles of unbroken ground, you'll see rooftops and water towers. But if you can simply accept the surroundings for what they are, the reward could be the biggest buck of your life.

Blue-Collar Trophy Hunting

How regular guys get big bucks.

By Scott Bestul

One of the best whitetail hunters I know is someone you've never heard of. He hasn't appeared on any hunting videos. He's not an elite member of some hunting pro-staff. He's never had his mug featured on an ad campaign or glossy magazine cover. In a hunting world chock-full of whitetail celebrities, my buddy is a nobody.

But I'd pit his hunting skills against any deer hunter I know, and I know some very, very good ones; names you'd recognize. I've hunted with the "experts" and I've hunted with my friend … and he's as good as anyone I've met.

Robert works for the city in a rural Midwestern hamlet. He doesn't own, lease or have exclusive hunting rights to any property, nor can he afford to hire a guide. He wouldn't be insulted if I referred to him as a classic "Joe Lunchbucket," a regular guy working a regular job who manufactures hunting time while the rest of his life—which includes work, family and community obligations—keeps chugging along.

Robert's tagged 10 trophy-class whitetails near his home during the past 10 years and added a couple more from other states during that time. And he's done it without losing his job, getting divorced, going broke or getting full of himself. Robert's passion is hunting big white-tailed bucks, and he's found a way to kill them consistently. Naturally, some folks—fellow hunters, mostly—are tempted to think Robert has some shortcut to suc-

cess: a secret hotspot, a special gift, maybe even a willingness to bend game laws. Not so on every count, as anyone from his wife to the local game warden will testify.

So just how does he find and kill big deer every year? Robert would be the first to insist there's no blueprint. But I do think he'd agree there are some concrete things hunters like him—I call them blue-collar trophy hunters—can do to increase their odds.

Set Realistic Goals

It wasn't long ago that anyone who shot a mature whitetail considered himself or herself as having bagged the "buck of a lifetime." After the lucky hunter nailed that one big one, their life settled back to normal, and they continued hunting deer the same way they had in the past. But during the past decade or so, we've heard more about the exploits of Myles Keller, Don Kisky, Stan Potts, the Drury brothers, etc., and have come to realize what was once a buck-of-a-lifetime for most hunters is now an annual event for others. Simply put, our expectations have been raised to the point that, once some hunters kill one big deer, they expect to immediately kill another, or a bigger one … just like those well-known hunters do.

Resist getting caught in this trap. First of all, whitetail hunting isn't a competitive sport and trying to kill as many (or even the same caliber of) bucks as a pro-staff hunter is like expecting to out hit Tiger Woods on the driving range. Full-time whitetailers have access to more and better hunting grounds than most of us, and some of the really blessed ones have nothing—nothing—on their schedules but hunting from September until January each year. Obviously, folks like us don't have that luxury.

Since the playing field isn't exactly level, hunters who set attainable goals for themselves will be less likely to experience frustration and more likely to be satisfied with the results when they do kill a buck. Trophy hunting is a time- and labor-intensive sport and for most of us, the challenge of fooling any mature buck is a tall one. Think hard about a reasonable expectation for this fall and be happy when/if you attain it.

So what's a reasonable goal? Only you can determine it, but try to match your expectations to your hunting experience, the amount of time you have to hunt and the quality of the land you have available to you. Remember, success is a relative term. I know men (blue-collar guys, too) who routinely pass up shots at 140-inch bucks while waiting for a true Goliath. Now, in the vast majority of the whitetail's range, a 140-class deer is about as good as it gets. But these guys live in primo country, have killed big deer before and want a monster or nothing at all. For a budding trophy hunter to set a similar goal would be ludicrous and result in nothing but frustration.

When I think of setting goals, I'm reminded of another skilled whitetailer: my cousin Scott. He's a fine hunter and excellent shot who has the skills to kill a big buck every year. But Scott's a self-employed carpenter whose job doesn't stop come fall.

Scouting and research can help you locate out-of-the-way big buck hotspots other hunters overlook.

Consequently, he's set a goal to take a nice buck every 3-5 years and so far, he's succeeded. Though less-skilled hunters with more time often shoot more bucks than Scott, he's content with his pace because he's set a reasonable goal.

HUNT THE GOOD SPOTS

Deer hunting has very few absolutes, but this much is certain: You can't kill a buck that doesn't exist. So the first step in killing big deer is simply finding them. If there are no mature bucks in your hunting area(s), don't frustrate yourself by waiting for them to show up. Instead, find another hunting area that does hold a few mature deer and then make the commitment to hunt there. This might require more time, research and possibly increased travel, but it's a necessary process.

If you're not plugged into where big bucks live, check out the record books of the Boone and Crockett and Pope and Young Clubs. Pouring over these record books will get you honed in on the hotspots in your area. Both clubs even produce maps now that show the number of trophy entries per county for every state.

Once you've identified the golden zones in your area, you're faced with a new question: Can a guy without a big wallet actually hunt such places? The answer is a cloudy "maybe." If you're thinking Texas, for example, forget it. But Iowa, a primo trophy deer state, can be a different story. There are still places in the Hawkeye State where you can access private land, and some of the state's public hunting areas are outstanding. My buddy Robert, for example, killed a monster 5x5 a few years ago in Iowa on a state-owned wildlife management area. The problem with any Iowa hunt, of course, is drawing a tag. One of the reasons Iowa has so many big deer is the state severely restricts nonresident opportunities.

Thankfully, there are other options. These come in the form of "sleeper areas" that, due to less publicity, nastier terrain and/or lower hunter numbers, produce big deer but are frequently overlooked. How do you find such spots? Through research and ingenuity. I won't draw any maps, but I will provide a couple concrete hints. Much of northern Minnesota, for example, consists of huge tracts of timber that most sportsmen fear to tread, and as a result, contain huge deer. Similarly, prairie states such as Nebraska and South Dakota have all the elements needed to grow huge bucks ... but many hunters ignore such terrain because they don't know how to hunt in open country, which is why the deer continue to grow old!

HUNT WHEN IT'S HOT!

If all blue-collar hunters share a common woe, it's limited hunting time. This makes nailing down the prime windows of opportunity that elevate the chances for success difficult. Since we don't have an unlimited supply of vacation days, scheduling the few we do get should coincide with the peak move-

Early- or late-season hunting (top and bottom) can provide just as many big buck opportunities as the rut (middle).

ment times of mature deer. If you need to schedule your vacation dates a long time in advance, consider the following three peak periods.

Naturally, the best time to kill a mature buck is during the weeks just prior to the rut. Mature bucks are the most active during the breeding season, and hunting them during the rut simply maximizes your effort. For example, when I first hunted the prairies of western Kansas, I made several calls before my trip to determine when the best breeding activity occurred. Two hours on the phone helped me nail down the two best weeks, so I scheduled my five-day hunt for the middle of that period. I saw more mature bucks during that short hunt than I would have during two complete seasons back home!

Take every opportunity you can to learn about how deer use your hunting area. Putting together all the pieces of the puzzle makes for hunting success.

If you can't hunt during the rut, schedule your hunting time during September or December. Early fall finds bucks still in their summer feeding patterns, often with other members of their bachelor group. By December, most bucks become serious about eating again, making them vulnerable at prime food sources. And because these time frames are often neglected by hunters, access to prime private ground is better than it is during the rut, when everyone wants to be out there. If you're hunting public ground, count on less competition as well.

LEARN YOUR LAND

One of the most talked about and least accomplished aspects of shooting big deer is scouting … at least among frustrated trophy hunters. The guys who kill big deer every year are scouting all the time. Robert, for example, could probably ignore most of the farms he hunts for a year or two and still shoot big bucks because he's simply dialed into how the deer bed, feed and travel on those properties. But every spare minute Robert has is spent walking the land, hunting for sheds and glassing bachelor groups of bucks. As he'll tell anyone who'll listen: "You can never know too much about how deer, especially big ones, use a property. I'm always looking for more pieces to the puzzle."

Naturally, frequent scouting trips are easier to pull off if you're hunting close to home. For out-of-state safaris, extra effort and ingenuity are necessary. If I know I'm going to hunt an area the next fall, I'll schedule a late winter or early spring weekend scouting/shed hunting blitz in the area. Arranging a spring turkey hunt in the area is another way to do some pre-season scouting (and hopefully kill a gobbler, too). While such short forays won't tell you everything you need to know, you'll at least get a strong glimpse of the land and be far better off than you would be by walking in cold come fall.

Minus a scouting trip, get your hands on aerial photos or topo maps of your hunting ground long before your hunt and then learn how to properly read them. If you're looking for a source of good topo maps and aerial photos, there are several Web sites (accessible through www.hunt-ingclub.com) where you can download, customize and create maps of any area in the country for a reasonable subscription fee. Short of visiting the actual area, I can think of no better way to scout ground than studying topos and aerials.

PRACTICE WITH A PURPOSE

All the scouting and hunting effort you devote is meaningless if you can't shoot the buck you've been scouting when it comes time to do so. Of course, misses are a part of hunting and even the "experts" miss deer now and then. But it's amazing how few hunters devote the time necessary to become proficient with their guns and bows. You don't have to be an ace marksman, you just need to be able to deliver the goods in that tension-packed, high-adrenaline moment when a big buck appears.

Summer is the perfect time to start shooting. Make a short shooting session part of your daily schedule several times a week if you're a bowhunter, and once a week if you'll hunt with a firearm. Start simple, with backyard, close-range shooting that just gets you intimate with your hunting tool. As the summer progresses, try to simulate hunting situations by shooting arrows at 3-D targets or shooting your gun at ranges that allow for longer shots. With a couple months practice under your belt, putting that broadhead or bullet into the deer's boiler room should be an almost thoughtless process, which is

just as it should be when that wide-racked monster finally appears.

CONCLUSION

Will following these steps ensure a trophy for a hopeful blue-collar trophy hunter? Of course not. Chasing big deer is a process full of hard work, endless commitment and plenty of uncertainty. But as Robert and my cousin Scott have proven, success is still within the reach of men for whom whitetail hunting is just a hobby, and not a job.

The hunt has many rewards, but making your shot makes everything perfect. Shoot often and practice with a purpose to be ready for "the moment."

REALITY WHITETAIL HUNTING

At its base, whitetail hunting is simple. Here are the keys.

BY TOM CARPENTER

*E*ven as I near a half century's worth of deer seasons, sleep comes grudgingly—if at all—before opening day.

But now, resting quietly in my sleeping bag, a string of whitetail dream hunts parades through my thoughts. Picking an approved rack from a ranch full of big South Texas bucks, trusty A-Bolt in hand. Tracking a Saskatchewan bruiser through fresh snow and taking him at twilight with my muzzleloader. Waiting alongside a frigid Iowa fenceline for the big 10-pointer that trotted past and then fell to the "whump" of my slug gun. Spending a golden autumn patterning deer during morning and evening treestand bowhunts in the imaginary wooded ridges behind my home, waiting for the buck that I want.

Beep-beep. Beep-beep. Beep-beep. The portable alarm clock ends my slumber.

Dream over. Opening day! I shuffle over to the shack's woodstove, toss in a couple chunks of popple and rub my eyes. Nice dreams. But not reality. This is reality: an old shack in the woods. Three good friends. Sixty-five acres and some strategically placed stands. Some deer around; maybe a buck, too.

Pulling on long johns, I think: In exactly two weeks I'll be rising for another state's opener and looking at a parallel reality: two friends' farms, 8 miles apart, one 260 acres and the other 200. Good deer country, but not premier. Some company in the field.

If your realities are like my dreams, you're lucky. But who has the dollars, land access and/or time to experience hunts like those? We read about them, but is that your whitetail hunting reality? It's not mine.

Maybe you're saving for a special hunt. Me, too. But until then, and after, there's a lot of whitetail hunting reality to deal with. Limited land—a farm or two, a lease or hunt club with friends, a chunk of land that you own, maybe public land. Limited time—we all need to work for a living and keep a family happy, too, so we have to count our beloved days in the woods carefully. Limited deer—habitat that is probably good but not necessarily crawling with deer to pass up as you wait for something "better."

So what can you do to increase your odds of success, given that you don't have all the money, land or time in the world to hunt?

Here's my reality whitetail hunting checklist. It focuses on firearms hunting, but applies to bowhunting, too. These are just common sense and effective strategies, techniques and tips—ideas that can make success happen for the average hunter. You and me.

BE THERE

In the end, a successful hunt requires one simple strategy: that you are in the field where you can shoot a deer. Even if it seems like the deer are gone from the acres that you hunt. Even if the weather is bad. Casual hunters overlook this fact; they are the ones who go home without venison.

I have yet to shoot a deer from my couch, or

Use mini-drives to move deer when the action is slow. But get in quietly, then go slowly. The idea is to move deer around, not out of, your area.

there's a deer for every 4 acres, or, theoretically, one within 140 yards of me at all times.

That's what I tell myself when the action is slow and I'm wondering if I'm crazy to be hunting so hard. Do some similar math for your hunting spots. You'll stay out longer and hunt harder.

INSTANT SUCCESS

This relates to attitude: You can be having a miserable hunt one moment, and five seconds later it can be one of your greatest. Think back to some of the deer that you've shot. Action unfolds quickly. Always be ready for something good to happen. And if bad things happen, don't give up.

A couple years ago, I sat through a blustery and uneventful morning until about 10 a.m., when a group of does loped across a hayfield toward my stand. I leaned against a hickory tree and tried to squeeze off a shot at the lead deer as she paused to test the wind. "Click." I shucked in another shell. "Click." Bad firing pin. Seven white tails flagged goodbye as I cursed my slug gun.

I walked a half-mile back to the truck, retired the slug gun, screwed a rifled choke tube into my little grouse gun and returned to my stand, determined to hunt out the day. During the late afternoon, the wind died down, and a twig cracked behind me.

I hadn't lost hope, and the shotgun was at my shoulder when a spike buck stepped out 20 yards away. "Boom!" And to be honest, there was another "boom" because I missed as he stood but rolled him on his second bound, when it was more like shooting at a grouse. In eight seconds, the day went from bad to great. I was there to make it happen.

the diner in town, or the warm seat of a pickup truck. If you want to be low-key and leave the woods, fine. But if you're serious about getting a deer, be out there where things can happen.

Dress right and be ready for an all-day stay. Carry a day pack with enough food and water for the day, and extra clothes and disposable body and hand warmers.

ATTITUDE

Whitetails are incredible hiders, which means that there likely are deer very close to you at any given time.

Fifteen to 20 deer live year-round on one of the farms that I mentioned; my farmer friend sees them in the fields on summer evenings. With maybe 80 acres of hiding cover on the place,

HUNT HARD, HUNT RIGHT

That's my pep talk. If you're a reality whitetail hunter, your effort and dedication—being out there, thinking positively and hunting hard and with your heart in it—will be the primary reasons why you either get a deer or go home empty-handed.

Now let's talk a few details. Stick to the simple here, too. Gadgets, gizmos and fancy tricks have yet to bring a reality whitetail to me, anyway.

KNOW AND LOVE YOUR GUN

Sight-in your firearm. A magnificent whitetail (they're all magnificent) deserves this respect and a clean kill. You deserve to miss if you don't shoot before the season. But knowing your rifle, shotgun, muzzleloader or bow will also help your attitude and confidence in the woods. One shot, one fleeting chance, is the only link between you and the deer that you've been dreaming about. Make it count.

Late summer is the perfect time to conduct this necessary part of the hunt. Sight-in before other fall hunting seasons occupy your time. Relax. Have fun with it. There's no pressure now. And don't get wigged out about ballistics and splitting hairs (see "Reality Sighting-In" on page 75).

Throw a bullet or slug through the barrel again before the season to be sure that you're still "on."

SCOUT RIGHT

I won't tell you that scouting is unimportant. But don't traipse around and spook deer away from your hunting area, especially as the season draws near. Set up your stands months before the hunt. If you're hunting a limited amount of land, chances are good that you won't be adjusting their position that much anyway.

Within a month of hunting season, do your spotting and scouting from a distance—from roadways or with binoculars. If possible, use the landowners' knowledge and sightings to tell you where the deer have been living and moving; this traditionally has been my best "scouting" of all.

One chance may be all you get. If you sight-in and then practice shooting, one chance is all you will need.

HUNT SMART

You know your hunting land better than I do—where the deer hang out, how to best hunt the terrain. But this approach applies to all reality whitetail hunters: Always take a low-impact approach to your hunting. Be smart about hunting what land you have.

Select your stands carefully and have alternate places to sit for varying winds. Yes, you might have to "overhunt" a stand; not overhunting stands is a luxury for those who have huge tracts of land to hunt.

Should you do deer drives? That's your call. I will do them—mini-pushes describes the tactic better—when the neighbors are in town having lunch or watching a football game on TV.

The idea is to move deer around, not out of, your hunting area. One hunter pushes. Go quietly. Go slowly. Sneak. My dad was a pro at this. It would take him at least an hour to go 100 yards on a mini-push. But the deer that he moved never hightailed it—they just skulked around him in the woodlot and often enough he'd hear a "boom" from my direction and smile.

Now, I push for him, striving to move as slowly and patiently as he did. Bottom line? This plan keeps deer where you can hunt them and not over on the neighbors' property.

We love it when the other hunters in Cadiz Township do their big drives. The little acreage that we hunt benefits from an influx of deer as they escape and then filter back out to their home ranges later. Another reason to stay put and hunt hard all day.

MOMENTS OF TRUTH

Do you know what saves many deer, as many as any other hunter boo-boo? I do. It's ruining the opportunity for a shot before you can even pull the trigger. Jerking the gun up too soon. Or too quickly. Or too late. Or moving too much in the process.

For success, think S-S-S-S: Slow movements—Steady your aim—pick a Spot—Squeeze the rifle or release trigger.

An approaching deer is always a surprise. Try to control your emotions. You might only get this chance. Move slowly but deliberately to get your gun up. Move only when the deer is moving, or when its head is hidden. You'll never win a quick draw. Don't panic or you will surely lose the deer. Be patient, but shoot when the shot is good.

I still get excited while hunting, but this helps: Think "S-S-S-S"—slow-steady-spot-squeeze. Slow movements. Steady your aim. Aim at one small spot on the deer's chest; you know where. Squeeze the trigger, don't jerk it. These steps can turn critical moments of truth into moments of success and elation.

SIMPLIFY, ENJOY

If you get the idea that I'm not a new-age whitetail hunter, you're right. Other than dressing smartly (good gloves, hat and boots) for the weather conditions at hand, carrying a rifle (or shotgun or muzzleloader) that you trust and a good, sharp knife, what do you really need for successful whitetail hunting? Dedication and a few simple but sound strategies.

And don't let somebody else's standards—on inches of antler or whether there's antler at all—destroy your appreciation of any deer that you are good and lucky enough to take. Remember, this is reality whitetail hunting for real people. What matters is what you think, the record book in your memory.

A REALITY WHITETAIL

Back to opening day. I leave the shack early, reach my stand 45 minutes before first light, put on the extra clothes from my day pack and climb up. Minnesota's November chill creeps into my bones, but excitement keeps me warm.

A few shots ring out here and there at first light. I wait. It seems like an eternity. But the woods stay quiet. I had scouted last spring and had not touched this spot since, except to pass by on a grouse hunt. The light south breeze is just right. It feels good to hold my old rifle.

Hoofbeats in the leaves! As I turn slowly, he is

Reality Sighting-In

You can study ballistics tables for hours, fret over fractions of inches and shoot until your shoulder is raw. Or you can follow these simple sighting-in guidelines and take the pressure off.

- **12-GAUGE SLUG GUN.** With a rifled barrel and saboted slugs, sight-in 2 inches high at 50 yards; you can hold right on to 100 yards. With a choke tube or smooth barrel and regular rifled slugs, use the same sight-in but hold right on, out to only 75 yards.
- **RIFLE.** For woods and brush hunting, sight-in to be dead on at 50 or 100 yards. Either way, you'll be right on for any shot that you encounter. There's nothing like knowing exactly where that bullet is going in these situations. When longer shots are possible, sight-in to be 2 inches high (no more) at 100 yards. I don't care what caliber you're shooting, you'll be dead on at 200 to 230 yards with everything from a .270 Win. on up; that's plenty far.

- **MUZZLELOADER.** Use the shotgun guideline: 2 inches high at 50 yards. You'll be good out to 100, maybe beyond, but check first.

there, hidden behind some saplings. My rifle is halfway to my shoulder. Slowly, I raise it up all the

Reality whitetail hunting success is not measured in inches of antler, but rather memories of quality time spent hunting.

way. I can see his white throat patch and eye rings through the scope; I know where his chest is.

Twenty years ago, I would have shot. But now I wait, so long that my arms begin to shake. And then he trots on past, 30 yards out. Buckskin flashed between tree trunks. I hold off. At the last possible moment he pauses and then lies quietly on his side, and I realize that I'd shot.

I wait a few minutes, wondering if I am still dreaming. But I'm not. This is real. I climb down and walk over to the buck, smiling. The sun's first rays clear the popple and oak trees as I knee beside him and hold his thick little 8-point antlers, thinking—this buck makes me happier than any dream.

THE SNEAKY FEET APPROACH

Hunting whitetails on the ground.

By Bryce M. Towsley

The woods had been warm and dry for weeks, and every attempt at movement sent pulsing waves of noise to the deer that were lying quietly in their shadowed beds. There was little a hunter could do except sit and wait. But the days spent perched in a treestand overlooking nothingness were driving me mad. I felt like an interloper, a belly crawling bushwhacker. This wasn't the deer hunting I knew and loved. This endless waiting, this sneaky ambushing, it wasn't the way I believed deer should be hunted. Effective? Yes. Satisfying? Not even close.

When I began whitetail hunting 35 years ago, treestands were all but unheard of in the circles I traveled. The men I knew scorned them as they hunted on their two hind feet—bringing it to the buck and moving through his turf and hunting on his terms. It called on skills unneeded and unused in trees. Skills that demand a level of concentration, commitment and effort far exceeding any needed for treestand hunting. It might be a tougher way to fill a tag, but it's the style of whitetail hunting I've always loved most. The thought that I might pass an entire season perched in a tree like an over-weight possum was too depressing to ponder.

But with the snow came a change. It muted the woods and inspired the deer to move, feed and breed. It was the catalyst that made them act the way deer should during the late New England fall.

When I left the wood-stove warmth of my living room and entered the cold, gray, November dawn, six inches of glorious, perfect snow blanketed the earth. The air was thick and still, perfect for absorbing the sounds of an approaching hunter. As I started up the mountain to meet the daylight, for the first time that fall I felt like a deer hunter.

Two hours later, I descended the same trail with a nice buck following along on my drag rope.

Sadly, I must confess that in the far too many years since, I've come to embrace today's almost universal approach of hunting whitetails from stationary stands. In doing so, I've taken several bucks that were bigger than that 5-point, but none more satisfying. I'll not abandon those roots, and I make it a point of pride to never let a deer season slip by without spending several days hunting with my feet firmly on the ground. It reminds me of what it means to be a hunter, and it keeps me sharp and humble.

TRAINING YOUR EYES AND MIND

When you look at the big picture, it's hard to argue against the effectiveness of treestand hunting for whitetails. But for satisfaction it doesn't compare to hunting in amongst the deer.

With the demands of modern life, most of us spend 50 weeks a year in our human environment. All the while, the deer are living in the woods. It's foolish to think we can simply step out of our environment, into theirs and expect to kill them with ease.

Have you ever seen a deer that had wandered into a city? It's completely out of its element—confused and inept at survival. Often, it ends badly for the deer. We're not unlike that when we enter a deer's domain. Perhaps it's human arrogance or simply that we don't see it, but we rarely recognize or admit that we're not tuned into the woods. But then, there's no way we can be because it takes time to train our eyes, body and mind to hunt deer effectively.

Once again, we're adjusting to this weakness and the human condition when we hunt from stands. Because we're stationary, we're waiting for deer to come to us. We look for movement, something that our human habitat trains us for anyway. It's what our eyes are conditioned for every day, because the hazards that pose a threat to us are generally moving. For example, a moving bus can be dangerous, but one that's sitting still poses little threat. Most deer hunters never change from that mode, and for a stand hunter it works because the hunter is stationary and the deer are moving.

When hunting on the ground, you should still look for movement; sometimes you'll spot a moving deer before it spots you. But that will be the exception, not the rule. Usually, when you're on the ground and moving, by the time you see movement it's already too late. The deer is fleeing the scene and all you'll see is its white-tailed salute.

It's important to train and condition your vision to the woods. It's not easy to change the way we operate because it's so automatic and ingrained during our non-deer hunting lives, but it's important.

The key is to learn to see what's in the woods. Look for parts of a buck—the shine of his nose or eyes, the shape of his ear, an antler tine or leg. Learn to see textures. Know the difference between the hair on a buck and the bark of a stump, that an antler is smoother and different from a branch. You must be able to pick the woods apart with your eyes and positively identify what you're seeing. All this is different from what you do the rest of the year and from how you hunt from a stand, and it takes training.

It's not just your eyes that must be conditioned, but your mind as well. If you're thinking about something other than deer hunting, you won't see deer. You must block out the distractions and con-

Big bucks are masters at utilizing the heaviest cover to avoid hunters. Sneaking in at ground level can put you eye to eye with your quarry.

centrate on deer hunting. This is important regardless of the style of ground hunting you use.

Unless you're tracking, most ground hunting will fall under the heading of "still-hunting," which is a term for slipping through the woods looking for deer. Most articles about still-hunting tell you to move slowly, which is good advice as far as it goes. But then the author usually spoils it by following with some kind of formula like, "You must move no more than 100 yards in 2 hours and 15 minutes." Or, "Never take more than three steps in any given 26-minute period." Or, "Always take steps exactly 19.5 inches long, particularly if the moon is in the third quarter or if ..." Enough!

HUNT SMART

There's no magic formula for still-hunting, only to think and use your head. You'll learn more from watching deer move through the woods than anything else. They don't follow any formulas, they simply react to the conditions. Sometimes they move along at a pretty good clip, other times they'll stand as still as a stop sign for an hour or more. They're simply interpreting the situation and reacting accordingly. Do the same when you still-hunt and don't worry about counting steps. Moving 100 yards in two hours might be a good strategy if you're in a thick cedar swamp that's full of bedded deer. But if you're crossing open hardwoods that are as devoid of deer as the ballroom at the Las Vegas Hilton, it's not going to do anything but waste productive hunting time.

Walking quietly through the woods is a conditioned skill. You must change the cadence and pace of your steps and also change the way you place your feet on the ground. Watch how deer walk and strive to become like the animal yourself—to blend with the rhythms of the woods.

Slow down, be aware of what's on the ground and how you'll use it to your advantage. You must walk on a variety of ground and terrain conditions to learn how to react to each one. Experience is the best and only teacher here. Something my grandfather told me long ago has helped as much as anything else. "Look at the deer tracks and watch where the deer walk," he said. "They know the woods better than you ever will." When I'm in doubt about the path ahead I look for the deer tracks and trails. They've never been wrong.

Learn to roll your weight onto your foot from the toe back and to "feel" what's underneath. Never allow yourself to be off balance so much that you can't react to a stick that's about to break. You must be able to instantly remove your weight from that foot, pick it up and place it in another location. That means you'll need to not only slow down from your careless "city" walking style, but you must also shorten your steps. By taking shorter steps, you'll maintain your center of balance between both feet so you can shift your weight to either leg.

Learn to "snake" your way though the woods so you can avoid

branches by twisting your body a little. Movement will always tip off a buck to your presence, but rapid or jerky movement will alert them sooner.

Hand movement is a big giveaway to a buck, particularly if you're not wearing gloves to hide the unnatural color of your skin. The only thing you should be moving when deer are close are your eyes and head. Moving your head is a necessary compromise to spotting a buck, but it should be a slow, smooth and methodical movement.

Stand vigilant against the demons of boredom. If you allow them to visit when you're hunting from a treestand you might still take a deer. Even if you're not paying attention you're likely doing little to spook a buck and if he's belligerent enough to demand that you notice him you'll probably get a shot. But if you grow bored and careless while ground hunting, it's all but inevitable that you'll not only stop paying attention, but that you'll also become careless about noise and movement as well. Another mistake bored hunters make is walking with their heads down, looking at the ground and not for deer. You can watch the ground with your peripheral vision most of the time, looking directly at it only when necessary to sort out a problem. Keep your eyes up, look ahead and keep them moving.

Ground hunting is hard and requires more of you mentally, and you cannot allow a moment of inattention. You must draw yourself in, focus and concentrate on seeing the buck before he sees you. The odds are in his favor.

A whitetail taken afoot creates a special satisfaction.

"PLAN A" FOR OPENING DAY

Hunt hard on day one for your best chance at a whitetail.

BY TOM CARPENTER

Whether you love it or loathe it, opening day is your best opportunity to shoot a deer during this fall's gun hunt. Opening day can at once be the most delightful and frustrating time of any firearms deer season. Many factors contribute to the great potential of opening day: more deer in the woods, unpressured and uneducated deer, plenty of hunters to keep animals moving and the excitement of just being in the woods deer hunting again.

But the opener can be frustrating, too. The blessing of hunting pressure is also a curse; you're not alone in the woods. Shots ring out everywhere, yet no deer come your way; did your deer get shot? And deep down you're torn—excited to get a deer but afraid your season might end too soon. Of course, hunting season isn't over if opening day flops. But the first day is your best chance to get a deer, so you might as well make it count. Ask yourself the following questions to prepare your attitude, hunting strategy and gear, then meld all three factors into a "Plan A" you can stick to for opening day success.

Hunt hard and be ready for a shot at any moment.

ARE YOU HERE TO SHOOT A DEER?

It's amazing how many opening day gunners don't plan on shooting a deer unless it's a huge buck. I say to each his own, because that attitude lets some deer live to come past my stand. More problematic is the hunter who hasn't decided what kind of deer meets his opening-day standards. The thoughts go like this: "Here comes one. Are the antlers big enough? It's awfully early in the morning. That's not a fawn but is it a big enough doe? I think I'll hold off and use my antlerless tag later. Well maybe not ... " and before you know it the opportunity is gone.

Hunter indecision and hesitation saves oodles of deer each year—deer that move on, hunker into their hidey holes and are never seen again.

I've regretted passing up legal deer because of opening-day cockiness, but I've never regretted taking the first legal deer that came along. This common man's suggestion: Look at opening day as just another day in the deer season of life. Who cares if the season's only a minute or hour old? It's just an extension of last year and a precursor to

The Numbers Don't Lie

Opening day is the best chance you'll have of getting your gun season deer, as shown in these statistics from a sampling of states.

STATE	PERCENTAGE*
Pennsylvania	.47%
Wisconsin	.40%
West Virginia	.38%
Missouri	.37%
New York	.36%
Michigan	.35%
Utah	.31%
Arkansas	.22%

Percentage of total gun season harvest taken on opening day.

next year. Shoot your deer, then enjoy the woods, relax at camp by the light of day, do little drives for other hunters in your party and simply enjoy your success.

Be sure to make a decision on what type of deer you want to shoot before heading into the woods. That way, you're not hemming and hawing and regretting a "don't shoot" decision days later when you're still in the woods and wishing you'd pulled the trigger when you had the chance during opening morning.

ARE YOU PREPARED TO HUNT ALL DAY?

If your answer is "no," fine. But you're exponentially decreasing your chances of success. If your answer is "yes," I'm betting you're going to kill a deer—or have a good opportunity—on opening day.

You probably won't shoot a deer at the crack of dawn. Yes, it does happen, but the follow-up hours—all the way to sunset—are just as full of potential. It's 8:30 in the morning. You're a little cold, a mite bored. Stay put! Every other hunter in

the woods is feeling the same way. Let them get up, mosey around and move a deer in your direction. Be tough. Grit your teeth. Count to 1,000 and then do it backward. Do whatever you can to avoid getting up and moving without a plan, which turns you into a deer dog for everybody else.

Switch stands if there's another strategic spot you like. But get there quickly and stay there, because the mid-morning hours are prime time. Deer move now through midday, often on their own, trying to sneak back to their core ranges after being shunted about early on.

Stay in the woods all day. Don't give up one hunting minute of your precious opening day. One year I had to, but I wouldn't let my dad, brother Larry or friend Ron do the same. My dad doesn't walk so well, so I left a little early to get the truck and drive through the farm fields to pick up the crew after hunting hours. I heard a shot on my long walk out, and when I returned, my partners were dressing out a good doe. She had exited a woodlot at the last minute of opening day's shooting light, and Ron nailed her at 80 yards with my old Ithaca slug gun.

SHOULD YOU SIT OR MOVE?

You've read this advice a million times. You know how to do it for the places you hunt: figure out where the hunting pressure is coming from, then take a stand on the deers' escape routes to those places, or in the places themselves, and wait for the action to come to you.

Gun Hunting 101, right? But how many of us follow the rule? Sit tight. All day. Change stands if you think it will help. I'll often move from field edges into thicker places by mid-afternoon, as deer finish traveling their regular routes and get to where they want to be. Avoid the "run around like a wild man" mentality—casting about here and there without a purpose, chasing shots and phantom deer. If you want to drum up some action, try to move deer when you're not pushing for (or interfering with) other hunters. During opening day, whitetails won't sit quite as tight as they do during the end of the season when you can't seem to find them anywhere.

Don't traipse around the deer woods on opening day (left). You'll only succeed in pushing deer to other hunters. Instead, sit tight and wait (right).

My motley little hunting group's best "pushes" come on opening day, at midday, when everybody else in the township is back at a farmhouse or diner eating lunch and we have the woods to ourselves for a few hours. It's fun to have a buck strung up when the hot-lunch guys return at 2 p.m. You don't have to be the world's greatest hunter. Just being there all day and hunting with a purpose and a plan—when you're sitting and when you're teaming up—will make the meatpole sag that first night.

ARE YOU PREPARED TO SHOOT?

You can do without lots of fancy gadgets and gear, even without an expensive rifle or shotgun. But the gun you do carry is your link to a deer and the one opportunity you might have on opening day isn't the time to be re-familiarizing yourself with it. Shame on you if you close the chamber on a shell or cartridge opening morning and think, "Well, it shot good last year. I haven't shot it since. Ah hell, it's still zeroed in. Yep. I'm ready."

You owe this to any deer you attempt to kill: have that gun sighted in and ready. Do it now, not at the last minute. If it takes only one shot to confirm you're still "on," great. But throw a few rounds through the barrel anyway. Handle the rifle or shotgun a bit and shoot from positions other than a bench. I've never shot a deer from a bench rest. Then clean the gun, throw another bullet or slug through the barrel (shots through clean barrels can become fliers), and you'll be set.

And line up your ammo—the right stuff—before opening day. It's simple but true.

One year long ago we were hunting with my Uncle Alvin and one of his friends. Alvin shot a couple slugs early on opening day and then discovered his backup ammo, bought in haste the day before, was 16 gauge and not the 20 gauge he needed! Uncle Alvin was a persuasive man and talked his friend Robert into going to town for the right slugs, while Alvin hunted with Robert's gun. Uncle Alvin was a lucky man, too—he shot a deer with Robert's gun while Robert ran the errand! You might not be so persuasive ... or lucky.

IS YOUR GEAR UP TO THE CHALLENGE?

Don't wait until the day before the opener to organize your gear. Start early. Make a list, cogitate it a little bit, slash unnecessary items and add details when they pop into your mind. Make preparation and anticipation a fun part of the hunt. Avoid eve-of-the-opener scrambles. They're no fun and a good way to forget important items.

I've spent years trying to figure out how to manage what I carry into the woods. I started out as a pocket stuffer and looked like an orange Michelin man. When fanny packs came into vogue, I'd stuff one to the brim and hang extra clothes off the back; but then I had to hitch up my pants all day. I moved to a daypack and that's perfect for the all-day stand hunting I do in central Minnesota. I can carry a lot of "stuff" and not really bother my hunting because I only have to wear the thing out to my stand and back. But in the farm-country hunting I do in Wisconsin and Illinois, I have to be more mobile. So I'll carry only what I really need—shotgun, slugs, clothes on my back, knife, license, tag, binoculars—and stash a daypack with extra clothes and other niceties somewhere convenient. It's never too far of a walk to get the pack, since my hunting acreage is limited.

Pack something substantial to eat. Forget about candy bars; they'll give you a temporary sugar high but won't fill you up. Bring some sandwiches, fruit and a few granola bars or cookies. Forget about potato chips and other fatty snacks—they'll make you gassy and you'll smell bad to deer. Avoid drinking pop. Instead, drink water or Gatorade, because it will hydrate you, which is important when the weather is cold. Speaking of cold (and other weather extremes), be ready for them. If you're cold, wet (or even too hot), hunting will be miserable and you won't stay out long.

The author with a good buck taken on a long opening-day sit. Packing light but right, and waiting with confidence, will pay off on opening day.

'PLAN A' WORKS

I climbed into the treestand well before first light, excited for the opening day ahead. The temperature hovered in the single digits, but I was dressed for the occasion. My strategy was simple: wait until dark. The rut was at its peak, opening day hunter movement would prod some additional deer movement and a crunchy little skiff of snow meant walking up on a deer would be impossible. I waited. I shivered. I gritted my teeth. But I wanted to shoot a deer, so I waited some more.

By 11:30 a.m.—after 5½ hours on stand—no deer had shown. But November's sun had warmed the brushlands a little bit, so I was comfortable. My stomach yearned for some food from my daypack, but this was midday prime time so I made myself wait. Brown flashed way out in the popple brush! I eased my rifle up as deer legs trotted toward me and then stopped. A bush started shaking. I made out the shape of a deer—must be a buck—thrashing brush. He continued his patrol, antlering a couple tag alders as I tracked him with the riflescope. When he stopped and turned broadside to rub another sapling, I shot. He got wobbly before I could bolt another cartridge into the A-Bolt's chamber, then fell over.

When I reached him, it was high noon. He was sleek and beautiful, and shreds of bark hung from his knobby little 5-point antlers. My season was over but that was fine with me. This was just an extension of all the cold days I'd suffered through on that stand last year, and life is one big deer season. Plus, the boys would be coming back from lunch soon to help me with the long drag!

Opening day success can happen in a heartbeat. So stay engaged in the hunt—looking, glassing, and hands on your rifle, shotgun, or muzzleloader so you're ready when the opportunity comes.

TOP 10
RUT-HUNTING MISTAKES

The rut isn't always a slam-dunk time to kill a good whitetail. Avoid these costly mistakes.

BY BOB ROBB

Chuck Jones is one of the best whitetail hunters around. For many years, we've hunted deer together, with me as the "hunter" and Chuck as the videographer, filming segments for TV shows and video series. Jones seems to know where the deer will be, regardless of the time of year or conditions at hand. That makes him a handy guy to have around.

One year, when hunting the pre-rut near his western Kentucky home got difficult, it started us thinking. Everyone assumes that the pre-rut and rut periods are slam-dunk times to shoot nice bucks. As we all know, however, even rut-hunting can turn cold.

During supper one evening, Jones, Harold Knight, David Hale and I sat around and wondered what we might be doing wrong. Hale, in his quiet manner, summed it up. "Just because the rut is supposed to be on doesn't mean that it's necessarily easy to take a good buck," he said.

How true that is. In the end, Jones and I managed to shoot a respectable 8-pointer on camera. We got our TV show, but more important, we learned a lesson in humility. Just because the rut is occurring doesn't mean that you can forsake the basic tenets of deer hunting.

With that in mind, here are the Knight & Hale team's list of the 10 most common mistakes that many whitetail hunters make when the rut is hot but their luck is cold. How many of them do you make each season?

1. HUNTING THE SAME SIGN TOO LONG.

"A lot of guys don't scout much and are satisfied with finding a single fresh scrape or a big, fresh rub," Hale said. "They then bet the success of their entire hunt on that one sign post paying off. The problem is not necessarily hunting scrapes too long, but hunting over the same one too long.

They forget that some scrapes are visited only at night; some are rarely, if ever, visited after they're made; and only a few are worked on a regular basis. They forget that

Although a big rub like this might get your heart racing, it doesn't guarantee that you'll see the buck that made it.

If you can find does during the rut, the odds are good that you'll see bucks, too.

you have to stay flexible and go with the flow, regardless of the season."

2. HUNTING WHERE YOU SAW BUCKS A MONTH AGO.

"During the rut, forget about where you saw bucks last month," Jones noted. "It's better to hunt where the does are, because that's where the bucks are, or are going to be shortly. If there are no does where you saw a good buck before the rut began, you can be sure that there won't be one there now."

3. HUNTING AREAS THAT ARE TOO THICK.

Instead of hunting in the thickest cover possible, Knight recommends hunting the edges of thickets so that you can see, and get a shot at, deer when they move past your stand. "Thickets are great places to find deer," Knight said, "but you have to be able to shoot them when you see them. Hunt the edges and be patient; sooner or later you'll get your opportunity."

4. NOT HUNTING DOE POCKETS.

Knight is a firm believer in hunting food sources

all season, but especially during the rut. "Preferred food sources tend to concentrate the does into little pockets," he said. "And sooner or later, one of them will come into estrus. I want to be there when she does. That's when the action gets fast and furious."

5. NOT ELIMINATING THEIR SCENT.

"Just because bucks become less cautious during the rut doesn't mean that they're stupid," Hale said. "And big does never are. You have to maintain cleanliness and complete scent control at all times in the deer woods. That includes your body and clothing."

6. NOT USING DEER CALLS ENOUGH.

The rut is the best time to call a buck in, using a grunt call or doe bleats. "This is the time of year that hunters need to be calling, because there is a high probability that a subordinate buck will respond to their grunt calls," Hale said. "I also do a lot of blind calling, because the deer are roaming and might be nearby at any time of day."

7. Not Clearing Enough Shooting Lanes.

You need several shooting lanes this time of year, because bucks are roaming more, and therefore will often come from unanticipated directions. "How many times have you heard someone say, 'He came in behind me and I didn't have a shot'?" Jones asked. "I make sure that I have clear shooting lanes in at least three or four directions during the rut. By the same token, I try to keep my trimming to a minimum so that the area doesn't look like a manicured park."

8. Not Hunting All Day.

Making sure that you have several shooting lanes available is important, especially when you don't know where a buck might appear during the rut.

"It's been written about for years, but people often forget that during the rut a big old buck can be seen roaming just as easily at noon as he can at dawn and dusk," Jones said. "This is probably the No. 1 mistake that rut hunters make. Forget about going back to the lodge for lunch or a nap.

Instead, get ready for action between 10 a.m. and

It's the middle of the day, but this big buck is on the trail of a hot doe. You'll never see him if you're home eating lunch.

2 p.m. That's when I've shot a surprising number of my biggest bucks."

9. Not Paying Attention To Equipment.

Sure, it's the rut and you're in a hurry to get into the woods. But, as Hale notes, if your equipment isn't in A-1 shape, or your firearm or bow isn't sighted in, you're defeated before you start. "Because it's the rut, more people hit the fields running, but many of them pay too little attention to their equipment, and specifically to their hunting implements," Hale said. "Be sure to sight your gun or bow in, and make sure that the gear in your daypack is in good working order."

10. Not Making An Effort To Hunt Different Areas.

"Most of us get comfortable hunting places that we've become familiar with," Hale said. "Heck, that's half the fun of a deer hunt. However, your old, faithful stand site this year just might not produce. I always try to have at least two backup honey holes that I can go to when my favorite stand isn't producing. It pays big dividends to stay flexible and hunt where the deer are, not necessarily where you want to hunt.

THE 10 BEST DAYS FOR A TROPHY BUCK

Peak breeding isn't the best time to shoot a rutting buck. Think earlier.

BY GARY CLANCY

Vinny was a disillusioned hunter. While he'd always longed to hunt big bucks in the Midwest, Vinny was from New Jersey, and he wasn't a rich man who could hunt whenever and wherever he wanted. Like most of us, Vinny worked to support his family. And putting aside a few grand for his hunt-of-a-lifetime in western Illinois was no small feat. But he pulled it off. So when we arrived in camp, no one in our small group was more excited than Vinny. When our outfitter, Mike Pavlic, showed him photos of the four big bucks hunters had taken the week before, Vinny became ecstatic! Nevertheless, four days later, with only two days of hunting left before he'd return home, Vinny looked like someone whose dog had just died.

"I don't understand it," Vinny said. "I asked Mike before I booked when the peak of the rut was, and he told me it was this week. But all I've seen are young bucks. And it isn't just me. The rest of you aren't seeing much for big bucks, either. I'm tellin' you Clancy, I don't think this area is all it's cracked up to be. I doubt the big bucks are even here. Those guys last week got the only big ones."

The 10 days prior to peak rut are ideal for hunters who use estrous scents, decoys and rattling.

"Oh, the big boys are here," I reassured him. "I've hunted this area for the past four seasons and I can vouch for that. The problem is the big boys are busy tending does right now. They don't move much when they've got themselves a girl. There's no reason to. The best thing to do is keep hunting from dawn to dusk and hope you can intercept one of the big boys when he's between does. Keep your spirits up, Vinny, because it can happen in a heartbeat."

"Let me get this straight," Vinny questioned. "You're telling me right now is peak rut, but this isn't the best time to be here? I've read the peak of the rut is prime hunting. What gives?"

What gives is this: Except in a few instances, "peak rut" isn't synonymous with the best hunting, as many hunters assume. It's a term hunters and wildlife biologists use to refer to the period when the bulk of breeding is accomplished. Although the peak of the rut isn't a bad time to be hunting for big whitetails, it most often plays second fiddle to the 10 days prior to it.

Mileage is the primary reason this is true. Your odds of seeing a big buck increase in correlation to the number of miles that buck puts on his

The author shared a camp with these proud hunters during this magical 10-day stretch. Hunting went from cold to hot literally overnight.

odometer during shooting hours. At no time during the deer season does a buck log the number of miles he'll accumulate during the 10 days leading up to peak rut. A mature buck is one busy animal during that hectic period; new scrapes are pawed out and dozens of established scrapes are checked and freshened on a daily basis. Also, searching for does and determining the readiness of each is a full-time job. And that job requires the buck to stay on the prowl almost constantly. Then, too, there's the occasional battle with a competing buck. It's an active period in a mature buck's year and, in my opinion, the best 10 days of the season to be in the woods.

In contrast, mature buck movement during peak rut is minimal. Once a buck finds a receptive doe, he'll sequester her in a place where he can protect her from competing bucks. In hill country, this place is often the head of a gully. Farm country bucks have learned to take their does out into the middle of wide open sections of harvested crop land, so they can see a potential rival buck approaching at long range. The buck will hold the doe in this private place and breed with her. Once the buck senses the doe is no longer receptive, which could happen 12 to 24 hours later, he'll abandon her and search for another estrous doe. In most areas of the country, with the sex ratio heavily favoring does, it usually doesn't take long for a buck to find another hot doe. The process is repeated until every doe has been bred. When all

is said and done, a buck doesn't cover nearly as many miles during peak rut as he does during the 10 days prior, and less movement means fewer opportunities for hunters to make contact with a buck.

Of course there are exceptions, places where the buck-to-doe ratio is well balanced. Texas, especially ranches in South Texas, which are intensely (and expensively) managed for producing mature white-tailed bucks, afford excellent hunting during peak rut because there's competition between mature bucks for available does. I've encountered similar situations while hunting in Saskatchewan and Alberta. There are similar "pockets" scattered around the country, but they're rare. If you're fortunate enough to hunt one of these places, then I certainly wouldn't discourage you from planning your hunt for peak rut.

FUN, FUN, FUN

Not only does the 10-day period prior to peak rut offer the best chance for seeing a big buck, but hunting during this stretch offers more fun than any other time of the season. The reason is because rattling, calling, decoying and using scents are most effective. During this period, I've rattled up 13 bucks in one morning and had seven bucks at my decoy in one day. On one memorable early November morning in western Wisconsin, I watched eight different bucks respond to my combination of buck grunts and doe bleats. Deer scents are also more effective during this 10-day stretch. During another early November hunt in Minnesota, I had four different bucks follow a scent trail I'd laid down to my stand before the sun had been up an hour. But I slipped a sharp broadhead through the lungs of the fourth buck and ruined the party.

To take full advantage of this period, I hunt all day and strongly urge you to do the same. I can't begin to count the number of big bucks I've seen between 10 a.m. and 2 p.m. I don't think it's a coincidence these are the same hours when many hunters take a midday break.

Picking The Right Dates

Now that I've convinced you, hopefully this year you'll take a week-long vacation during that magical 10-day peiod just prior to peak rut. But how do you determine the exact dates?

One way to find out this information is to call a white-tailed deer biologist in the state you're going to hunt. Ask the biologist for the peak rut dates and be sure to let him or her know what part of the state you'll be hunting. A few states, mostly in the South, have peak rut dates that can vary up to a month for different regions.

Here are my recommendations for the 10 best days for each state.

But I must warn you that if the weather is unseasonably warm, as it's been for recent seasons, then everything I've said in this article goes right out the window. When it gets hot during this period, bucks, which are all decked out in their winter coats, have no choice but to stay in the shade during the day and do their carousing at night. Daytime movement is then confined to a paltry couple of hours at first light and sunset. As you might suspect, our odds of success drop dramatically when the weather turns hot. But if the weather doesn't throw you a curve, this 10-day period will likely provide you with your best opportunity for getting a crack at a good buck this season.

Clancy's 10 Best Deer Days

MID-OCTOBER TO MID-NOVEMBER

Delaware: *Oct. 31-Nov. 9*
Georgia (north/central): *Nov. 3-12*
Idaho: *Nov. 3-12*
Illinois: *Nov. 3-12*
Indiana: *Nov. 7-16*
Iowa: *Nov. 6-15*
Kansas: *Nov. 3-12*
Louisiana (southwest): *Oct. 8-17*
Maine: *Nov. 5-14*
Maryland: *Nov. 3-12*
Massachusetts: *Nov. 5-14*
Michigan (U.P.): *Oct. 22-31*
Michigan: *Nov. 1-10*
Minnesota: *Oct. 31-Nov. 9*
Missouri: *Nov. 3-12*
Montana: *Nov. 3-12*
Nebraska: *Nov. 3-12*
New Hampshire: *Nov. 3-12*
New York: *Oct. 31-Nov. 9*
N. Carolina (upper coastal): *Oct. 31-Nov. 9*
Ohio: *Nov. 7-16*
Oklahoma: *Nov. 7-16*
Oregon: *Nov. 6-15*
Pennsylvania: *Nov. 5-14*
Rhode Island: *Nov. 1-10*
Washington: *Nov. 3-12*
West Virginia: *Nov. 6-15*
Wisconsin: *Oct. 27-Nov. 5*

MID-NOVEMBER TO MID-DECEMBER

Arkansas: *Nov. 11-20*
Colorado: *Nov. 8-17*
Connecticut: *Nov. 12-21*
Georgia (south): *Nov. 11-20*
Kentucky: *Nov. 8-17*
Louisiana (northwest): *Nov. 8-17*
Mississippi (north): *Dec. 1-10*
New Jersey: *Nov. 8-17*
New Mexico: *Nov. 6-15*
N. Carolina (Piedmont): *Nov. 11-20*
N. Carolina (lower coastal): *Nov. 16-25*
N. Carolina (Mtn.): *Nov. 28-Dec. 7*
North Dakota: *Nov. 8-17*
South Carolina: *Nov. 16-25*
South Dakota: *Nov. 8-17*
Tennessee: *Nov. 11-20*
Texas (Hill Country): *Nov. 8-17*
Texas (west): *Nov. 24-Dec. 3*
Texas (south): *Dec. 3-12*
Virginia: *Nov. 9-18*
Wyoming: *Nov. 8-17*

MID-DECEMBER THROUGH JANUARY

Alabama: *Jan. 11-20*
Florida (north): *Dec. 24-Jan. 2*
Florida (central): *Dec. 30-Jan. 8*
Florida (south): *Jan. 15-24*
Louisiana (east): *Dec. 25-Jan. 3*
Mississippi (south): *Jan. 4-13*

Deer Disclaimer

I've crawled out on a proverbial shaky limb here. Many of you will plan your vacation around the recommendations I've made. I'll be a hero to some and a real chump to others. But I'll gladly shoulder that burden because I firmly believe everything I've written here.—*Gary Clancy*

FINE-TUNING THE RUT

Understand the rut's intricacies to find hunting success.

BY CHARLES J. ALSHEIMER

After years of spying whitetail rut behavior through the lens of a camera and from a bowhunting stand, I view this ritual as the best to be found in the deer woods. Because my career revolves around whitetails, my biological clock, so to speak, is set for mid-October.

Though white-tailed bucks scrape, rub and chase does, the does create the rut. Therefore, my hunting strategy revolves around pursuing mature white-tailed bucks as they interact with the doe groups that frequent the area I hunt.

A white-tailed buck's rutting switch is thrown around October 15 north of the Mason-Dixon Line. For the next 30 to 45 days, he develops an ever-increasing urge to breed. And from the end of October until about mid-November, whitetails are in the chase phase.

Those once-untouchable bucks let down their guard and become vulnerable to the careful hunter. Once the breeding gets going, the same bucks become a bit tougher to hunt because of the does. So, the best window of opportunity for hunting rutting bucks is that two-week period just prior to breeding. In order to fine-tune your rut-hunting approach, knowledge of buck and doe behavior during this time is essential.

BREAKING IT DOWN

For the most part, bucks hang in bachelor groups during September, bedding and feeding together. As October arrives, testosterone drives bucks to begin scraping and checking out the does around them. Feeding is less of a priority. Also, their range begins to increase.

By mid-October, a few does will come into estrus. The smell of hot does causes bucks to go into a frenzy, and the competition for the right to breed with the first does of the season is keen. Now the scraping and chase phase of the rut kicks into high gear.

By November, a white-tailed buck gets a final infusion of testosterone. At the same time, a doe's estrogen level reaches its apex, setting the stage for her to come into estrus. For bucks, scraping, rubbing and chasing take higher priority than food or rest. And aggression is peaking.

THE MOON MATTERS

Contrary to popular belief (past research included), the majority of does do not breed at the same time each year.

More than 70 percent of the does in our Northern research project came into estrus off the second full moon after the autumn equinox, known as the Hunter's Moon. From seven to 21 days after the Hunter's Moon, the majority of the breeding takes place. For this reason, the breeding dates will vary each year, depending on when the Hunter's Moon occurs. By knowing when the Hunter's Moon falls, a hunter can determine with reasonable accuracy when the scraping, chasing and breeding are most likely to happen. Peak scraping and chasing will usually occur during the 10- to 14-day period preceding peak breeding.

A lot of scent communication takes place at scrapes. But the reliability of scrape hunting is a fleeting few days. Don't hang your rut hunt all on one scrape.

When the breeding time becomes full-blown, nearly every hot doe has a buck in her thicket. Because an estrous doe is receptive for up to 72 hours, a buck will stay with her and possibly breed her several times during this period. With the does now in charge, the only buck movement to be found is when a doe decides to move about to feed or a buck is in search of another doe.

RUT HUNTING STRATEGY

A whitetail's range can be broken into three zones: feeding, bedding and the area in between that I call the transition zone. If hunting pressure isn't severe, the transition zone is where I ambush most of my rutting bucks. There are five reasons for this:

• Mature bucks seldom frequent feeding areas during daylight hours.

• If they do, there are usually does nearby, and the scene can resemble a fire drill when the chasing starts.

• With several deer in the feeding area, you often have too many eyes to contend with before the moment of truth arrives.

• I believe it's best to stay out of the bedding area in order to keep a mature buck from changing his habits.

• The transition zone is where much of the rutting sign will be found and where a buck is most vulnerable.

Generally, a transition zone's size depends on how far the bedding area is from the feeding area. If a transition zone is thick or happens to be a natural funnel, your chances for success increase.

If conditions and habitat are right, a number of trails should pass through a transition zone. It's along and near these trails that I look for key rutting sign by mid-October. As the rut intensifies, three types of scrapes normally show up: boundary, secondary and primary. I pay little attention to boundary scrapes, except for checking the size of the tracks in them. Boundary scrapes are random scrapes bucks make as they travel about their range. They often show up along the edges of fields, fencerows, old roadways and creeks. So, as the name implies, they are along boundaries. Many boundary scrapes are made by yearling bucks as they try to figure out their first rut.

Secondary scrapes can offer excellent chances to kill bucks because they are generally found along well-used trails between the bedding and feeding area. In many instances, bucks make a line of these scrapes 20 to 50 yards apart. Because they are on trails, bucks will frequently freshen them.

The scrape of all scrapes, as far as hunters are concerned, is the primary scrape. The primary scrape is the true "watering hole" for white-tailed bucks. Unlike secondary scrapes that are placed on trails, primary scrapes are visited frequently by all bucks in the area and often have several trails leading to them. They are usually in thick cover where mature bucks feel secure.

DECISIONS, DECISIONS

Setting up an ambush over a primary or secondary scrape can be tricky. First, try to find a hot scrape as close to the bedding area as possible. By doing so, you'll be in a better position to intercept a buck visiting his scrape during daylight hours. With the majority of scrapes being made under the cover of darkness, it's important to be close to the bedding area in order to intercept a buck as it moves to and from the bedding area. If you set up too far from a bedding area during an afternoon hunt, the buck won't reach you before quitting time. The same applies for morning stands, though it is not as critical. During the chase phase—especially from the

As the rut heats up (left), even bucks that spent the early fall together engage in battle to determine breeding supremacy. The victor (right) wins the right to breed with receptive does.

Hunter's Moon to the last quarter phase of the moon—rutting bucks are active until midday. At least they can be if the temperatures are not abnormally high.

When hunting scrapes and rub lines, terrain and cover dictate where I hang my stand, usually 15 to 20 feet high, 25 to 60 yards downwind of the scrape. This is because mature bucks often scent-check a scrape from downwind during daylight. To conceal any movement, I go to great lengths to ensure that my stand is in thick cover. If the tree supporting the stand doesn't offer ample cover, I attempt to camouflage the setup naturally with evergreen boughs.

SOLID STAND STRATEGIES

One method I use to get a buck to pass by my stand is making scent trails using doe-in-heat scent.

If scent use doesn't draw a buck close enough, calling is my next choice. Because of their aggressiveness, rutting whitetails are very receptive to the sound of a doe bleat or a buck grunt. Usually, all it takes is a few soft bleats or grunts to get a rut-crazed buck within range. These calls can work throughout the fall, but the best response will come during the two weeks prior to breeding right on through the post-rut. You can call blind (with no deer in sight) or hit the call when you see a buck traveling past your stand out of range.

A call that can be especially lethal during the chase and breeding phase of the rut is a tending grunt. This grunt resembles a ticking sound. Not all commercial calls can make this sound, but the hunter equipped with one increases his chances of calling a buck to his location. Rut-wired bucks know that when they hear the tending grunt there's a good chance that a hot doe is nearby.

Though I've found calling whitetails to be more effective than rattling, no aspect of hunting during the rut is more spine-tingling than rattling in a buck. Once you've done it, you'll be hooked for life. Just like other types of calling, the best time to rattle is just prior to peak breeding when bucks are very aggressive. However, be forewarned. If the buck-to-doe ratio is more than three or four does for every antlered buck, rattling will seldom work. For best results, an area needs a tighter ratio and a fair number of mature bucks.

I use a relatively large set of real antlers and rattle aggressively using a three-step process. I limit the entire sequence to about seven minutes. It consists of rattling for about two minutes, pausing for 30 seconds, rattling for two minutes, pausing for 30 seconds, and rattling for two minutes. I often make a couple of doe bleats just prior to beginning my rattling sequence. The key is to make the sequence sound like there is a genuine knock-down-drag-out fight going on.

Fine-tuning the rut seems complicated to many hunters. But today we know a lot more about whitetails and the structure of the rut. The key for North American Hunting Club members is knowing what to look for and being able to hunt during that magical two-week period. That way you stand a chance of tagging the buck of your dreams.

K.I.S.S.
Method for Calling Deer

Getting your message across is easy.

By Gary Clancy

Even though white-tailed deer use a wide-ranging vocabulary to communicate with each other, you don't have to learn their entire language to get your point across. Calling whitetails is like visiting a foreign country. You don't need to speak fluent Spanish to enjoy a vacation in Mexico, for instance. Learn the Spanish words for food, water, hotel and bathroom and you will get along just fine.

I've been calling deer for a long time, which does not make me an expert, but it does make me experienced. I use the Clancy K.I.S.S method of calling, K.I.S.S. being short for Keep It Simple, Stupid. Here are the four deer vocalizations I rely upon. They will attract white-tailed deer no matter where you hunt.

I use a variable-tone grunt tube for 90 percent of my calling and one of those "calls in a can" for the other 10 percent. I've also learned to make these four vocalizations by mouth just in case I forget my calls or one freezes up.

The Contact Grunt

The contact grunt is a whitetail's way of saying, "Hello." Bucks use this sound more frequently than does, and there doesn't seem to be any rhyme or reason to when or why.

Any time a buck is on his feet he is likely to make a contact grunt. If another buck hears it, he is likely to respond by walking over to check things out. There is no aggression involved, mostly just curiosity, I suspect.

The contact grunt is usually the best call to use during early pre-rut or post-rut. It is a very low-volume, short and soft grunt, so I use it mainly on bucks that are out of range but within sight. If the buck is walking in dry grass or leaves, wait until he stops before you call so he can hear you. Although bucks usually only utter a single contact grunt, I use as many as it takes to get the deer's attention.

Once you have the buck's attention, quit calling. Deer are not quite as adept at pinpointing the exact source of the sound as wild turkeys, but they aren't too shabby at it. If you keep calling once the deer is headed your way, it will lock right in on you. Remember, the contact grunt is soft and short. Uurrp.

Trailing Grunt

The first time I heard a buck making the trailing grunt I thought one of the farmer's pigs had escaped. But pigs don't wear heavy 10-point racks like the deer making its way to me did. I managed to miss the

You don't need to know the whitetail's entire vocabulary to successfully call in a deer. Learning a few of the basic sounds whitetails make during the rut will get your message across.

Mature bucks become very aggressive and territorial during the rut. If you can convince one that there is an intruder infringing on his domain, be ready for a close encounter.

will hustle over to get in on the action. When I'm using the trailing grunt to call to a buck that I have in sight, I will call only until I have his attention. But I spend more time "calling blind," when no deer are in sight. I use a string of 20 or more grunts while slowly rotating the barrel of my grunt tube in a 180-degree arc to mimic a buck on the move. The trailing grunt sounds like this: uurp—uurp—uurp—uurp-uurp-uurp.

THE TENDING GRUNT

There are those who will argue that there is no difference between the trailing grunt and the tending grunt, but I disagree. While it is true that a buck in the company of an estrous doe will often continue to make the trailing grunt, I suspect that this continuance is just a holdover from the trailing period. Once a buck actually has a doe where he wants her, which is usually in some thicket or nasty draw where he can keep her all to himself for the duration of her estrous cycle, the grunts he uses sound nothing like the trailing grunt.

A buck is most likely to make tending grunts when the doe is trying to get away from him—which seems to be a good share of the time—or when another buck shows up.

I use the tending grunt frequently during the rut. It is especially effective during those hectic days just prior to the first wave of does entering estrus. The tending grunt is also my favorite call when hunting over a deer decoy.

The easiest way to make tending grunts is to fire off a string of trailing grunts but with longer, drawn-out grunts mixed in with shorter ones. Put some emotion into the call. Remember, this is a once-a-year deal for whitetails!

A typical tending grunt goes something like this: uurrp-rrp-uurrp-uurrrrrp—uurrp-urp-rp-rp-urp-urp-uurrrrrrrp-urrrrrrp-urp....

There is one more facet of the tending grunt that deserves mentioning and that is "clicking." I

buck, but I sure had something new to listen for in the woods, and it wasn't long before I learned to imitate the sound.

The trailing grunt is a deadly call from late pre-rut through the breeding period. Bucks make this sound when they are trailing a doe in estrus. Sometimes the buck has the doe in sight, but more often he will be scent-trailing her.

The trailing grunt is no longer in duration than the contact grunt, but it is louder, repetitious and you can hear the anxiety and excitement coming through. Some bucks will grunt each time a front hoof hits the ground, others use it more sporadically. Some bucks on the track of a hot doe don't grunt at all. I suspect how vocal each individual animal is when trailing a hot doe depends upon his mood and the signals his brain is receiving from the scent he is inhaling.

When another buck hears a trailing grunt, he knows what it signals and, nine times out of 10,

THE DOE BLEAT

You can imitate a doe bleat on most adjustable grunt calls or you can purchase a mouth-blown call specifically designed for producing doe bleats. I sometimes use this sound when I'm trying to fill an antlerless tag. Does are attracted to a doe bleat. I also use the doe bleat to calm down deer that I have spooked on the way in to my stand. Many times, a few doe bleats will calm the alarmed deer down and allow you to get to your stand without further disruption.

Another trick is to use one of those "calls in a can" that make a doe bleat each time you tip the canister over. Mix a few doe bleats in when you are making either trailing or tending grunts on your grunt call. Quaker Boy markets the Bleat In Heat can, and the Primos can goes by the name of Easy Estrous Bleat.

Because you can blend the grunts with the bleats by using the two calls at the same time, this is a very realistic scenario. In fact, the largest buck I have ever shot at responded to a combination of tending grunts and doe bleats—but I don't want to talk about that. The memory of my arrow slipping just under the brute's chest is still too painful!

There is nothing scientific or complicated about calling deer. In fact, of all the critters that can be called, deer are the easiest in my experience. Get a good call or two, practice, and then use my K.I.S.S. method this season. I wouldn't be surprised if you become as hooked on calling deer as I am.

don't know if all bucks tending a doe click or not. I do know that of the bucks I've observed tending does only about 20 percent used clicking, but the other 80 percent could have easily done some clicking when they were not under my observation. I also know that I've gotten some mighty strange looks in hunting camps and at seminars when I've discussed this clicking thing.

The click is worth mentioning because every buck I have ever heard making clicks was tending a doe in estrus. This means that when an unattached buck hears clicking, he knows that there is a receptive doe in the picture. And all of the bucks I've observed clicking were mature bucks. If that interests you, learn to click on your grunt call. It's easy to do, just put the tube to your lips and say tick—tick-tick-tick-tick-tick-tick-tick.

BUCKS ON THE CUSP OF A STORM

Bad weather gets bucks moving. Hunt the storm out.

By CHARLES J. ALSHEIMER

That October was not kind to bowhunters in my home state of New York. Throughout the latter part of the month, archers sweltered through a prolonged Indian summer. Seldom were there any frosty mornings, and on most days hunters were forced into short-sleeved attire for an afternoon shift in their treestands. Needless to say, the heat brought daytime deer activity to a standstill. This trend continued until early November. Then things reversed for two days.

During the afternoon of November 3, it was obvious that there was a change in the air. Being a TV weather watcher, I knew that I was about to see the rut kick into high gear—compliments of a cold front from the west. Throughout the afternoon, deer were feeding in the fields, and it was clear that they knew a weather change was imminent. From what I saw on the Weather Channel and the handheld barometer that I carry, I knew it, too—only I needed technology to tell me.

I awoke the following morning to nasty conditions, the kind that encourage many hunters to turn off the alarm and roll over for another couple hours. Before dressing for the woods, I poked my head out the back door in the pre-dawn darkness. The ground was covered with an inch of snow and the wind was howling. I quickly dressed, ate breakfast and headed out the door. I wanted to get to my favorite bow stand before daylight. In spite of the inclement conditions, I believed that the passing cold front would ignite every local buck into a rutting frenzy.

My guess was right. During the first hour of light, I passed up three 2½-year-old 8-pointers as they passed close to my stand. Deer were everywhere, and for the first two hours I saw at least one deer every 10 minutes while swaying back and forth in my wind-blown perch. With the temperature in the high 20s and winds gusting to 25 mph, the windchill was turning me into an icicle. I wanted to leave several times, but continued deer sightings kept me hanging on. I tolerated the cold and wind for three and a half hours before heading back to the house to thaw out.

With the cold temperatures, buck and doe activity remained high for the rest of the day and the following morning. Then the fast-moving front exited to the east, the heat returned and deer activity reverted to a snail's pace. In spite of the fact that the calendar said that bucks should be rutting, I saw little chasing on and around our farm. In a span of hours, the woods went quiet as the temperatures climbed into the 60s. It was clear that Mother Nature was controlling the rutting switch.

WEATHER AND WHITETAILS
It's weather, more than any other aspect of their environment, that influences the behavior of

whitetails. Everything else being equal, weather determines a whitetail's bedding, feeding and movement activities.

Through the years, I've realized that understanding weather fronts, and the weather that precedes or follows, can mean the difference between success or failure in the deer woods. Aside from the basic necessities of survival, it's weather that causes an increase in whitetail movement when natural conditions prevail. I'll even go so far as to say that once a deer hunter understands the various hunting techniques, his application of them to weather systems will be a key to success. Certainly, learning how to hunt weather fronts isn't the only key for a hunter, but the weather systems that accompany a front might dictate the hunting methods used during a particular day.

During the course of a year, weather causes all kinds of disruptions, and frenzies, in the way that whitetails feed and move. Knowing this has made me more of a weather watcher during the past 15 years, especially during deer seasons. I watch the Weather Channel during hunting season to find out what's happening in the Midwest and Southeast so I'll know what to expect in the way of weather. I also keep track of the barometer to see if it's falling as a front moves closer.

BE A WEATHER WATCHER

Unlike humans, whitetails and other wild creatures have built-in mechanisms to alert them to impending weather changes. Whitetails are able to detect when the barometric pressure is falling, even if the sky is clear. They know when things are in the process of changing, and their feeding habits increase dramatically before bad weather arrives. An example of this is described in my opening.

From experience, I've concluded that whitetails typically move more when the barometer is moving—up or down—than when it's steady. I've noticed whitetails don't like to move when the barometer is low and steady. During this time, you'll usually find periods of high humidity with fog, haze, rain and wet snow making up the weather system. When this happens, whitetails become secretive, especially in periods of dense fog.

Several studies have been conducted on the effects of

Whitetails have the unique ability to sense weather changes before they happen and will increase their activity level before an impending storm.

barometric pressure on whitetail activity. Illinois biologist Keith Thomas found that most whitetail feeding occurred when barometric pressure was between 29.80 and 30.29. When the barometric pressure is falling or rising through this range, deer activity should be at its greatest. So, be a weather watcher to ensure that you have the upper hand.

HUNTING THE FRONT

It's important for hunters to realize that it's not the sudden drop in temperature that often accompanies fronts that causes whitetails to head for the thickest cover. Rather, it's the unsettled weather associated with the leading edge of the low-pressure front that causes movement, with the greatest deer movement occurring if the barometric pressure drops rapidly. With few exceptions, little movement will occur once the front arrives. Then, as the front passes through and the weather returns to normal, whitetails and other wildlife start to move again in search of food.

When the front finally moves on and the skies clear, deer hunters will almost always find some of their best hunting. If a hunter is in the woods within a few hours of the front moving out of an area, the hunting can be fantastic.

Unfortunately, few whitetail hunters have the flexibility to take to the woods when weather conditions are best. Most hunters must wait for a day off from work and hope that they hit it right, unless of course, they know how to hunt during various weather conditions. When fronts are coming and going, many strategies can be successful for hunting whitetails.

If you know that the barometer will be falling and a low-pressure system is coming, your best bet is to hunt the feeding areas, scrapes and natural funnel zones. It's during this time that whitetail activity will be high prior to the front's arrival. Once the front arrives, stand hunting might be futile as deer activity will be at a minimum, unless the rut is full blown. It's during these lows (when the storm has arrived) that still-hunting might be at its best. Usually, the rain or snow will cover any noise that's made underfoot. Also, the wind associated with a storm or low-pressure system will help to cover any noise that you might make. Even swirling wind can be used to your advantage because whitetails will often have difficulty locating the source of human scent. If you've ever had a desire to be a still-hunter, this is the time to try.

When the lows are present, whitetails will most certainly be in thick cover or in their traditional bedding areas. Storms force them to seek thick cover and they won't leave such areas unless they're forced to. It's truly a time that the hunter must hunt the bedding areas to be successful.

Once the front has begun to move out of an area, wildlife activity increases as the weather returns to normal. Whitetails will then move to feeding areas to catch up on the feeding frenzy for two or three days, depending on how long the storm lasted. It's during this time that many deer hunters find their greatest successes.

WEATHER FRONTS AND THE RUT

If the rut is combined with weather fronts, whitetail hunting will be at its finest. When the front is either coming or going, the does are busy feeding. This, coupled with the continual movement of bucks, makes hunting exciting. Over the years, I've found hunting scrapes particularly productive when these two factors line up. If possible, hunters should stay on stand all day because buck activity will be continual. Midday can be particularly productive, with bucks cruising their territory in a non-stop fashion. When a full moon occurs in late October or early to mid-November, hunting opportunities increase even more, as the full moon will trigger bucks to go into a rutting frenzy, providing that the air temperature is within seasonal ranges.

Warm temperatures will shut down rutting activity in a heartbeat. A prime example of this occurred a few years ago, when the United States experienced its warmest fall on record. No matter who I talked to, the story was the same: warm temperatures caused the rut to be strange. Of all weather factors, air temperature is perhaps the most powerful influence on daytime deer activity and should be scrutinized when looking at weather fronts and what that front might do to deer activity.

One of the reasons why I'm not too fond of guided whitetail hunts to other parts of the country is because of the impact weather fronts and temperatures have on deer hunting. Usually, such hunts are short—four to six days in most cases—so the hunter is at the mercy of what nature deals him in the way of weather. Because of the short duration, unfamiliar country and less flexibility to adjust hunting tactics, such hunts can be frustrating. I've been on great guided hunts and others that I'd rather not remember.

BE A FORECASTER

A smart deer hunter prepares to be weather forecaster in the field. One doesn't necessarily have to be near a radio to forecast the weather. Regardless of whether I'm in my office, working in my whitetail research facility or in the woods hunting, I carry a pocket-sized portable barometer. Made by Oregon Scientific ((503) 639-8883) for hikers and mountain climbers, the tool proves valuable in predicting what will occur with the weather.

Sighting a ring around the moon is a visual way of telling that the barometric pressure will be falling and signals a change in the weather 18 to 36 hours before a front's arrival. Ice crystals in high clouds that typically precede a storm cause this.

In addition, I attempt to identify cloud types to tell whether a storm front is coming. Altocumulus clouds are often a sign of unsettled weather or an approaching front. Generally they're seen as an extensive sheet of regularly arranged cloudlets, white and gray, and somewhat rounded. If they're found gathering on the north or northwest horizon and accompanied by a south or southwest wind, it's an indication that the barometric pressure is falling. When this condition exists, whitetails will usually be in a feeding mode.

Hunters who pay attention to changes in the weather give themselves a marked advantage while in the woods.

Five Keys to Hunting the Storm

- The majority of whitetail activity occurs when the barometric pressure is moving between 29.80 and 30.29.
- When the barometric pressure is falling and a low-pressure system is coming, your best bet is to hunt feeding areas, scrapes and natural funnels.
- When a front arrives and a storm is in process (rain or snow), stand hunting might be futile with deer activity at a minimum. Still-hunting the bedding areas shines during this time.

- Once the storm is over, try to be on stand ASAP—within an hour if possible—as deer will be moving to feeding areas.
- When the storm passes and the barometric pressure begins to rise, bucks will be in feeding areas and on the move. If temperatures are seasonal during the two to four days following the storm, deer activity will be high—especially if the rut is in full swing.

Deer activity spikes on the "bluebird day" after a storm. So get out there and hunt!

When the front actually arrives, the cloud cover will usually be in the form of stratus clouds. These clouds produce drizzle and snow, and are gray and ominous looking. When these clouds appear, whitetail activity diminishes in most cases and trying to hunt deer from stands will be almost futile, unless, of course, the rut is at its peak.

On the other hand, clearing skies signal that a front might be on its way out. Also, slight breezes from the north or northwest and high and scattered cumulus clouds can be confirmation that a front is leaving the area. When this happens, whitetails will again be on the move to their food source.

If more whitetail hunters studied weather and weather fronts as much as they do scents and the rut, success rates would no doubt be higher. Mastering whitetail hunting techniques is a challenge, but one thing is certain: knowing how to hunt the weather fronts can add precious memories to the hunting experience.

THE LOST ART OF PUSHING DEER

Team up with a partner and give whitetails an old-fashioned "nudge."

BY TOM CARPENTER

Deer hunting has gone solitary and sedentary—sit alone and wait a lot.

Teaming up with a partner or two to move deer into each others' gunsights used to be a great way to hunt whitetails. Doing a little push (deer go where they please and are never really "driven") is still a great way to kill a buck. But land ownership patterns and hunting rights situations have changed. Most of us just sit and wait these days.

Even when not constrained by fences and boundary lines, today's deer hunter seldom partners up and moves out to hunt deer. But no matter where you pursue whitetails—large tracts of public land or limited private acreage—you can have a chance at putting your tag on a buck without running him out of the territory … if you hunt right.

Make a little push when the deer aren't moving on their own in daylight, when you're tired of sitting, or when the hunt is nearing its end. Sneak into a good deer hiding area and nudge the whitetails out of their beds to get them moving toward a strategically positioned poster or posters.

A low-impact push lets you take some control over your hunt's outcome. Knowing the intricacies of the lost art of pushing deer may inspire you to leave that stand, recruit a partner or two, put on your hiking boots, and make something happen in the deer woods this season.

HOW: THE ART

A good push is not nonchalant. It is a carefully planned scheme with posters sneaking to crossings and other escape routes undetected, and pushers getting into position furtively and then sneak-hunting through good deer cover to nudge the animals toward the posters.

A push is not a deer drive. It is done with only two to four hunters. And the process is art more than science: knowing the kinds of places deer like to hide, where you hunt; identifying the crossings, trails, escape routes and other subtle passages the whitetails use to get to safety; and moving the deer.

• POSTING. For posters, there is art in learning how to get to ambush spots without being detected by deer, then waiting without movement until the pusher(s) come through. Getting there quietly without being scented, staying put—and shooting straight—are the chief skills.

There's more to the posting art. Realize that whitetails will rarely if ever exit cover in a neat and orderly fashion, going straight away from the drivers. Today's bucks and does are too educated to plod blindly ahead. They go where they think they'll be safe, often on a direct route that isn't in front of the pushers. In fact, sometimes my posters are to the sides of (or even behind) the pusher's basic direction of travel.

• PUSHING. For the pusher, there is art in taking

If you're the pusher, get right into the cover and HUNT. Always be ready to shoot, as your chances are good.

the right attitude and hunting at the right pace. I call the preferred method a sneak-hunt. This plan moves the deer out slowly at a walk or jog, offering a better shot opportunity to posters. And if you push thoroughly and carefully enough, you can have as many shot opportunities as your posters get. (See "Pushing for Safety" sidebar.)

Hunt with your shotgun, rifle or muzzleloader ready for action at all times. If you work the cover right, a modern whitetail will be mighty surprised to see you coming through the very same place he's hiding, and he may offer a ridiculously easy shot, even at a standing target.

You have to go right into the cover and actually hunt. No logging trail cruising or ridge running. Pushing deer is not an autumn stroll. Get in the thick stuff where deer are; otherwise, they'll just let you walk on by.

Don't worry much about stealth, but do focus on being slow and thorough. Walk through those raspberry canes. Kick that brush pile. Crawl through that thornapple thicket. Wade through those brambles. Stop awhile. Backtrack and re-cover real estate you've already worked. Wander a bit. Don't walk a straight line. Stop again and just

look. Deer will either sneak out far ahead of you—maybe toward your posters—or hold tight and offer a you a shot right there.

Given my druthers, I always choose pushing over posting. Maybe it's because I'm an old rabbit hunter at heart, but I just love working the brush and making something happen. The only difference is that now I'm hunting a cotton-tailed deer.

WHERE: SMALL COVERTS

Pushing deer is most effective in relatively small pieces of cover. With only two to four hunters participating, these little and often out-of-the-way coverts, to borrow a bird hunting term, are more manageable to work. These are also the places whitetails go when the guns start booming.

Keep your push short. The farther a deer gets from his bed, the more chances he has to take an alternative route and pass through your poster(s) unseen.

I limit our small family pushes to a few hundred yards—a quarter mile at most—in the hilly farm-and-woodlot country of southwestern Wisconsin. I've seen and hunted similar countryside from there to southern Minnesota, Iowa, Illinois, Indiana, Missouri, Pennsylvania, New York and Tennessee. Deer country isn't that different from North to South to East to Midwest, and a good little push can work anywhere.

Even if you hunt the big woods, think small. You'll be most effective if you select pieces, patches and sections of terrain, then work them one by one. Don't try to push a huge piece of cover all at once, or tackle any distance over a few hundred yards.

Because pushing deer is an art, and because you know your hunting country better than me, you pick the places to push, the spots for the posters, and the routes the hunters will take to get to their starting and posting positions without the deer seeing, hearing or smelling them. That said, here are a few ideas for setting up some pushes.

•   **WOODLOT.** Post one, two or three hunters at various escape routes, often off to the side of the pusher's direction of travel. Try letting one hunter trail the pusher, or post at the back door where the push begins.

•   **BIG WOODS.** Post one hunter in the middle of good deer cover. The pusher sneak-hunts a circle around him or her. The circle can have a radius from as little as 40 or 50 yards to as much as 100 yards out, depending on how thick the cover is. Move on, trade jobs, and do it again. You can also hopscotch in the big woods, with posters skirting the cover to be hunted before taking up positions, and then the pusher working through.

•   **MARSH, GRASSY FIELD OR CRP LAND.** Get posters in position with great stealth, beyond or below a rise, hill or other obstruction that will prevent the deer from seeing them. The pusher then moves in, thoroughly covering the area. Deer will exit right away, or sit tight until you step on them.

•   **DITCH OR FENCELINE.** Sneak a poster to the end of the cover. Position one or two hunters off to the side, along escape routes or in cover the deer might head to. Pusher moves slowly through.

Pushing for Safety

Small pushes are more effective than big gang "drives." Pushes are also safer for hunters. But there are still important safety rules to follow.

•   Posters do not shoot in the direction from which the pusher is coming. Wait for the deer to pass into a safe shooting lane.

•   Pushers can shoot, but never in the direction of a poster. This requires a little thinking before pulling a trigger—time lost but time well spent.

•   Posters stay put until the pusher is completely done with his or her work. This way, even if late action erupts (as it often does when skulking whitetails are the quarry), all participants are where they are supposed to be.

The quarters can be close on a push. That's part of the excitement, but also part of the responsibility to hunt safely. If you can't shoot

Before shooting, take a moment to think about where your partners are.

at a deer for safety reasons, let it go. Watch where it goes. The way I see it, then you get to plan another campaign and try again!
—*Tom Carpenter*

With or Against the Wind?

When it comes to the wind and how it relates to planning a push, a wide variety of opinions are pontificated from bar stools and deer camp easy chairs every year. Do I push with the wind at my back or in my face? Should posters be upwind (where deer like to go but also can smell you) or downwind (where deer are less likely to go but can't smell a waiting hunter)?

I prefer to keep things simple. On rare autumn days when wind is nonexistent, you can ignore the concern altogether. When the breeze is at gale force, it's pretty much a non-factor too, because the deer can't use it anyway. It's those fickle, erratic winds in the middle that get perplexing.

At these times, whitetails tend to escape by heading into the wind, where upwind danger can be smelled. So place a poster downwind and to the side of a crossing. But I have seen many bucks (they seem to do it more than does) head off with the wind, using their eyes to look for danger ahead and their nose to keep track of pursuers behind.

I usually push into the wind, especially if I think the cover is such that I might be able to get a shot. Pushing with the wind can be effective because it spreads your scent ahead of you and moves deer out early toward posters. Pushing cross-wind is always an acceptable compromise.

As you can see, I don't worry the wind factor to death when hunting with rifle, slug gun or muzzleloader. The firearms' range erases many of the mistakes that might be made. And while it is good strategy to consider the wind when planning a push, whitetails often don't follow the rules anyway.—*Tom Carpenter*

• **RIVERSIDE TIMBER.** Similar to hunting a ditch or fenceline, only on a bigger scale. Be sure to cover the back door. Concentrate on river bends where cover widens out.

• **ODD CORNERS.** Never underestimate a whitetail's hiding skills. When the deer disappear, try weird, out-of-the-way odd spots. I have shot deer in, or pushed them to posters, from: a brushy and forgotten farm implement graveyard in a gully 50 yards behind a barn; a fieldside patch (about the size of my bedroom) of black raspberry canes; a grassy swale in the middle of a cut cornfield; the stalks of a haphazardly harvested cornfield; brushy fencerows that look more like pheasant cover. The key element is surprise—posters in position out of sight, and a sneaky and thorough pusher who is suddenly just there.

SUCCESS AND SATISFACTION

In the end, pushing deer isn't rocket science. It's more like a simple art you fine-tune with each passing season. But pushing deer does require some knowledge of the country you hunt, a well-

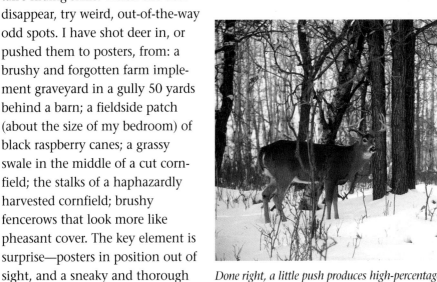

Done right, a little push produces high-percentage shots at deer slowly traveling past the poster(s).

Whether it produces a buck or doe, a successful push makes for great hunting camaraderie and memories that last a lifetime.

laid plan, some stealth in getting posters and pushers into position, and a thorough hunt to nudge the deer up and moving.

I love getting together with a partner or two to push deer for several reasons. One—it is an art, and there's precious little of that in our hardcore hunting styles these days. Two—it is effective. Dozens of deer have fallen victim to little pushes of my planning, over the last third of a century.

Finally, it's also about the camaraderie. Some of my fondest and most satisfying hunting memories come from working together in a small group like this—teaming up to get a deer (buck or doe, it really doesn't matter) for the meatpole.

And on the best hunts, the ones I think about most often and recall most fondly when I need to conjure up some whitetail memories, I wasn't even the one that pulled the trigger.

Making Shots

A good, gentle push produces a deer moving at a trot or walk as it evades the pusher and approaches a poster. Opportunities like this are better and safer than a deer "drive" animal fleeing at full speed.

When posting, be patient and try to wait for a standing shot. Whitetails will pause to check their backtrail and also preview what's ahead. Avoid shots at deer that are really booking. A yell or a whistle can sometimes stop a deer in its tracks for a quick shot. My brother Larry did just that on a big doe last fall, and one shot dropped her.

As a pusher, always be ready to shoot. Never sling that gun over your shoulder; carry it at-the-ready. You can connect! Sometimes it's a running shot. But often enough, I have had a deer, reluctant to leave the safety of the cover, take a couple bounds and then stop to look around. If you take a step or two to one side, you can often find a shooting lane.—*Tom Carpenter*

One more step and he's yours. Are you ready?

PART III

Grow
Them

More and more whitetail hunters are buying or leasing their own hunting land these days. Either scenario is a major investment, and it's only natural to want a return on that investment. You may want big bucks, more deer ... or just to get any deer at all to start coming to your land! Whatever your goals, habitat management is the answer. Whether it's selective logging, a clear cut or, as we focus on in much of this section, food plots, you really can attract deer, keep them around and grow big bucks. It's hard work, but it's worth it on the lifelong journey of a whitetail quest.

CREATING GREAT FOOD PLOTS

They're easier than you think.

BY SCOTT BESTUL

The buck walked into the food plot as comfortably as my kids enter our kitchen. It was a full hour before dusk, but the clover growing in that small, remote field was a powerful dinner bell for the handsome 8-point. When I'd first spotted the buck, I stood slowly and grabbed my bow. With the buck's nose buried in the clover, I quickly looked at his antlers. Though only as wide as his ear tips, his beams were heavy and his tines arched skyward, indicators this might be the 3½-year-old buck I was waiting for. But as he fed closer, I studied his rack and decided to pass on the shot. Another year of good nutrition and this 2½-year-old would be much larger.

That hunt occurred several falls ago on a tiny food plot on my cousin's central Wisconsin property. Planted on a log landing (a small clearing where loggers pile timber), the ⅛-acre plot hardly qualified as a field. But by doing some minor tillage, planting some seed and tending the crop, my cousin had produced a food plot that drew whitetails like a magnet. The success of that first plot led to the creation of others scattered throughout the property, and each new food source has made his 400-acre woodland a better hunting ground than it was before.

The success of food plots on my cousin's property isn't an isolated case. With the growth of private land deer management escalating, interest in attracting deer and providing them with quality nutrition has

also risen. Food plots cannot only increase the number of whitetails on a given tract, they can also enhance the body weight of all deer and the antler growth of bucks. Food plots also give more "bang for the buck" than supplemental feeding and/or baiting, creating a steady, reliable food source that whitetails feel comfortable visiting. And, once established, food plots require less maintenance and expense for landowners than simply spreading corn or continually filling feeders.

TWO TYPES OF PLOTS

Make no mistake, sometimes establishing a food plot can be as simple as clearing a little ground

Neil Dougherty has learned that the best way to grow big bucks is to improve their habitat.

and sowing some seed. But to maximize use by deer and hunting opportunities for you, it's best to plan the location, size and purpose of food plots carefully. For advice on this topic I turned to Neil Dougherty, habitat consultant for NorthCountry Whitetails, a deer consulting firm in southwestern New York (call 315-331-6959, log on to www.northcountrywhitetails.com, also see sidebar on page 124). Neil and his father Craig own 500 acres in the largely forested hill country of New York's No. 1 deer hunting location, Steuben County. They've created a whitetail paradise on the property, constructing food plots in the rugged, mountainous terrain through an aggressive habitat management program.

"The best time to start thinking about food plots is during the winter, months before you start planting them," Neil said. "The first step is to get an aerial photo of your land and mark the known feeding and bedding areas and travel routes of deer, as well as the prevailing wind directions in the area during a typical hunting season. All these factors come into play when we think about establishing a food plot."

Neil divides food plots into two categories. "We call them either feeding or hunting plots," he said. "A feeding plot is just as the name implies: a place where large numbers of deer can visit to put on the pounds, usually after dark. These are large whitetail grocery stores—usually 2 acres in size or greater—and the location isn't critical because we don't hunt over them. In our heavily wooded terrain, we'll put a feeding plot wherever we can get one in. They require larger equipment to establish and maintain, so you need to place them wherever you have a road large enough to get a bulldozer in to build the plot, and a tractor to do the tilling and planting."

In more open and/or broken terrain, establishing a feeding plot requires less effort than it does in heavily wooded country, where access might be difficult and clearings few. The NorthCountry Whitetails facility

fits the latter description, and the Doughertys have learned how to make fields where there once was nothing but forest. "Actually, logging is a key way to create the openings and access roads you need," Neil said. "We've had our logging crews build roads for us through the property and make clearings where we've needed them. Of course, an active, aggressive timber management program is crucial for maintaining good deer habitat here, but the loggers have been a tremendous help in our food plot work, too."

Neil describes the second type of food plot as a hunting plot. As the name implies, a hunting plot is designed to attract deer during daylight hours with the intent of shooting one. Smaller in size than feeding plots and carefully situated to take advantage of natural deer patterns, hunting plots on the NorthCountry Whitetails facility are planned months in advance. "We look at bedding areas, travel routes and terrain and situate the plot where it will be most attractive to deer," Neil said. "I go as far as actually picking out an ambush site—a tree suitable for a portable treestand or a spot for a ground blind—during the previous hunting season. Then I visit the spot and drift 'wind floaters' (small, light wisps of fabric) for several nights so I can determine the prevailing wind. When the plot is finished, I want to know exactly where to situate my stand so I'm not detected by

The NorthCountry Whitetails facility is located in the forested hill country of southwest New York.

Carefully plan the location of both food plots and new roads before meeting with your logger.

any deer visiting the plot."

Since hunting plots are much smaller than feeding plots, they're easier to start and maintain. "We've found that for bowhunting, these plots should be no more than 1 acre," Neil said. "Our best size is about ¾ acre, and they can be as small as a logging road or log landing that receives enough sunlight (four hours to five hours per day) to grow the plants we want to

Sound Land Management

Landowners must recognize that food plots should be just one component in an overall sound land management strategy. For example, many sportsmen will pour thousands of dollars and countless hours into establishing lush food plots, but they refuse to harvest the timber necessary to optimize their whitetail habitat. This is a mistake Neil Dougherty sees frequently as he travels the country and visits clients. "Food plots are an excellent tool," he said, "but you need to maintain a lot of young forest for deer to give them not only bedding and security cover, but also to provide them with the woody forage they require at certain times of the year.

"I had one client who refused to cut trees on his property, but had more than 20 acres of food plots where he'd see only four to five deer feeding at any given time. I finally convinced him to harvest some timber and improve his habitat. In a couple seasons, deer sightings on his food plots skyrocketed, and his neighbor, who owned an apple orchard that was usually full of deer, complained he never saw whitetails anymore. My client was giving those deer everything they needed. He was setting a better table for them." For advice on harvesting

Mature forests like this one provide little forage or cover for deer.

timber for maximum wildlife production, Neil advises consulting a state or local forester.

Next, have some reasonable goals and expectations. "Our property in New York will probably never grow a Boone and Crockett Club buck," Neil said. "The quality of our land won't allow it. But I get tremendous satisfaction in making our deer better than they ever were. I get invitations to hunt all over North America for huge-antlered whitetails, but come November, I want to be on our family's property, hunting a 130-inch buck I helped get that big."—*Scott Bestul*

Grow Them   119

Building Food Plots on CRP Land

ew people realize the government actually encourages landowners to plant food plots for wildlife on lands set aside in the Conservation Reserve Program (CRP).

If you lease hunting land that's placed in CRP, your first step is to explain to the landowner how food plots will pull deer away from his farm crops and thereby reduce his crop losses. It's also a good idea to explain how food plots will benefit a variety of wildlife, not just whitetails. This could include wild turkeys, quail, pheasants, rabbits and more. I've found that landowners are almost always receptive to the food plot idea.

When conducting this meeting with the landowner, be sure you have aerial and topographical maps with you of the region. This way you can show the property owner the locations you're interested in. Be sure, if possible, to plant the food plots out of view of any road. This will help protect the wildlife, since any potential poachers won't be able to see what size bucks are present.

Your next step is to contact your county Natural Resources Conservation Service (NRCS), a branch of the United States Department of Agriculture. While the landowner will know the person he deals with at the NRCS regarding CRP land and will have the phone number, you can also find this information yourself by looking under either Government Offices, or U.S. Government Offices in the Yellow Pages. It might be listed as Agricultural Service Center under these office headings. In addition, if you're on the Internet,

Nutritious food plots help CRP bucks reach their highest antler potential.

you can obtain a tremendous amount of CRP information there. I type in www.in.nrcs.usda.gov for my home state of Indiana. Simply type in your state abbreviation in this address to open your state's Web site.

Once the NRCS is contacted, you and the property owner will need to set up a meeting

establish." While the initial clearing of a hunting plot is done by a bulldozer operator, much of the tilling, planting and maintenance can often be performed by using an ATV or small tractor. This makes hunting plots more affordable than feeding plots for the average landowner.

BREAKING GROUND
Unless you're a heavy equipment operator (or know someone who is), breaking the ground necessary to establish food plots promises to be the most costly phase of the process. Prices for bulldozer work vary according to region, but Neil says sorting through reputable operators in the Yellow Pages can yield results, as can chatting with a local

with them. Obviously, you want to do this during the farmer's off-season. This meeting is necessary to confirm that you are, in fact, the person leasing the land, and that the landowner approves of what you want to do.

The key is for you to be prepared at this meeting. Determine beforehand how many acres of food plots you'll be able to afford, the location you desire them to be in and what you want to plant. Have your maps along and highlight the proposed food plot locations. You don't want to waste the landowner's or agent's time by being unprepared.

Although I knew the CRP was highly receptive to wildlife management, I was surprised to find out how much CRP land you could actually plant in food plots. Limits differ by state, but my home state of Indiana allows up to 10 percent of the total CRP acreage on a farm to be in food plots. Specifically, food plots must be at least ¼ acre in size, but no more than 5 acres. CRP fields less than 5 acres in size can be planted entirely in food plots if they're surrounded by non-cultivated ground.

The NRCS prefers food plots to be located close to cover. This provides wildlife using the food plots with a quick escape should predators try to kill them. For deer hunters, this is a major benefit: You can place a treestand or ground blind in heavy cover and have whitetails in the food plot within easy shooting range.—*Brad Herndon*

Acreage Guidelines

*I*n order to plan the correct amount of herbicide, lime, fertilizer and seed for a food plot, you have to know its size. The following chart will get you started. Remember, for hunting purposes it's best to have a rectangular-shaped food plot that brings deer within shooting range of your stand.—*Dave Maas*

1 acre = 4,840 square yards
Examples: 20 yards x 242 yards or 40 yards x 121 yards

½ acre = 2,420 square yards
Examples: 20 yards x 121 yards or 40 yards x 60½ yards

¼ acre = 1,210 square yards
Examples: 20 yards x 60½ yards or 40 yards x 30¼ yards

⅛ acre = 605 square yards
Examples: 20 yards x 30¼ yards or 10 yards x 60½ yards

1/16 acre = 302½ square yards
Examples: 10 yards x 30¼ yards or 5 yards x 60½ yards

wildlife or soil conservation biologist about contractors they've used. "You can learn a lot about the person's experience just by talking with them and asking about their work on food plots or establishing fields," Neil said. "You want to be specific about your goals, and tell him you want to visit the site with him and describe what you want done." When asking for price quotes, Neil advises

it takes about 8 hours of work to clear and prepare a 1-acre field.

As mentioned earlier, another good, and often economical, source for food plot work is loggers. "Most properties could benefit from more aggressive timber harvest," Neil said. "And we've been able to trade the harvested lumber value for the costs of establishing food plots and roads with our loggers. With the heavy machinery they typically have, they can work quickly. And they appreciate being able to access the property on the roads they build, which will be around for our use for a long time."

How to Take a Soil Sample

Materials needed: clean plastic pail, spade shovel or soil probe, Ziploc bag.

Procedure: Remove soil samples in an "x" pattern over the proposed food plot. Depending on the size of the field, 10 to 15 samples will be required. Before removing a soil sample, scrape away any vegetation. The sample should be comprised of the first 6 inches of soil. If you're using a spade, remove a V-shaped wedge and then cut a thin slice of soil from one side of the hole. Place the soil sample in the plastic pail. Mix all soil samples from the field in the pail and then place about 1½ cups of this mixed soil in the Ziploc bag. You now have one soil sample that represents the entire food plot.—*Neil Dougherty*

Once you've located your heavy-equipment operator, visit the food plot site with him. "I like to have the boundaries of every plot flagged, so he knows the exact placement," Neil said. "It's not as critical with feeding plots, since they're larger and used primarily as year-round food sources and not specific hunting locations. But on the hunting plots you need even the brush piles placed just right. For example, you don't want a rim of brush around the food plot that the deer must circle as they approach. Instead, you want the deer to step easily into the food plot. We like to have the brush placed in three piles, with one right behind the stand tree (which is on the downwind side of the plot) so deer won't approach the field and smell you (see diagram on page 124). It's also important that the bulldozer operator understand you don't want him scraping the topsoil off the field when he's clearing trees and brush. He needs to 'roll' the brush and trees to the side, and a good operator can even shake the roots to knock the dirt off them and leave it on the site."

One often-overlooked potential food plot is a logging road itself, according to Neil. "They make an excellent hunting plot because they're so narrow. And it's surprising how much food you can produce for deer on a road. For every 1,000 feet of 12-foot-wide road you plant, you're looking at nearly a 1-acre food plot. Orientation of your roads is an important consideration for maximum seed growth and production, however. In the South, where drought and heat are a major concern, the best results will occur on logging roads running north to south. But in northern regions, where getting enough sunlight is your main goal, an east to west road will yield the best results."

WORKING THE SOIL

Once the brush and vegetation has been cleared from the site, it's time to prepare the soil for planting. Step one in this process is breaking up the soil enough to allow seeds to germinate. "How aggressively you need to work the soil depends on the soil itself and how well the bulldozer operator has worked it up when he created the plot," Neil said. "In many situations, a four-wheeler and a pull-behind disc will do the job well enough to work up the 3 inches of soil you need to get seeds to grow. Many landowners already have an ATV, and by adding a few quality implements they can have the satisfaction of doing much of the work themselves."

Landowners can often trade food plot building costs for harvested lumber value.

Naturally, rougher ground and larger plots will probably require heavier equipment. "That usually means a tractor and a three-point hitch-mounted plow," Neil said. "We're seeing more landowners deciding to invest in small tractors and other farm equipment just to work on food plots; they consider it another long-term investment in the property. But if the expense of owning a tractor is too much, you can often pay a local farmer to work the ground for you."

The next step is obtaining a soil test to determine its pH level. This measurement indicates soil acidity. Once you know the pH of your soil, you'll know how to treat it with lime and/or fertilizer before planting. "We recommend taking a soil sample for each food plot you intend to establish," Neil stressed. "One sample for the whole property will not be enough, as soil acidity varies from site to site."

A soil sample can be taken to your local Agricultural Extension office, Farmers Co-op or local feed/grain store. Once a laboratory analyzes your soil, it'll recommend how many tons of lime per acre must be applied to neutralize the soil based on the crop you'll be planting. Usually, 1 or more tons of lime per acre must be applied to change the soil's pH significantly. The lab will also recommend the proper amount and type of fertilizer to be added to the plot. Soil testing costs run from $8 to $20 per sample.

In most cases, raising the pH of the soil by applying lime will be necessary. "In very acidic soils you'll want to bump that pH up rapidly," Neil said. "Finely ground lime will react quickly and cause a fast rise in the pH. One good product for this is BioLogic's pHfertilizer, which is a combination lime/fertilizer that will raise the pH nearly one point in only 3 weeks. For example, if your soil has a pH of 6 (medium acidity), the application of pHfertilizer will bring it up to about 6.8 or 6.9 (near neutral acidity). It makes a huge difference if you want to see quick results. However, the pH will drain away just as quickly, but for many situations—such as when you're establishing/planting a food plot just prior to hunting season—that's OK.

"Basically, maintaining the proper pH in the soil is a constant battle. How much of a battle depends on your soil type; sand loses pH quickly, and clay maintains it more readily because it's denser. There are lots of factors working against you: Rain will wash away the lime you apply; deer will eat the plants that boost pH and rob your plot of the very nutrients you need. It takes patience and constant maintenance—we consider most first-year plots a loss and don't expect them to produce for a season or two. But if you keep at it you'll have a good and productive food plot that will grow the nutritious plants the deer will want to eat."

GETTING READY TO PLANT
In "Food Plot Strategies—From Seed to Success,"(page 127) we'll explain how to fertilize,

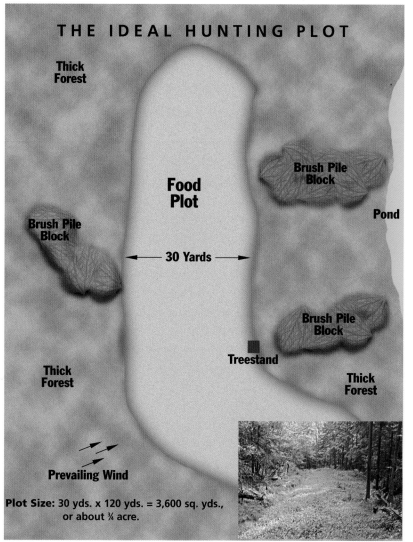

THE IDEAL HUNTING PLOT

Thick Forest

Brush Pile Block

Food Plot

Pond

Brush Pile Block

← 30 Yards →

Brush Pile Block

Treestand

Thick Forest

Thick Forest

Prevailing Wind

Plot Size: 30 yds. x 120 yds. = 3,600 sq. yds., or about ¾ acre.

With a little effort, logging roads can be turned into fantastic food plots.

When planning a hunting plot, strategically place head-high brush piles to funnel deer into the plot and near your stand.

plant and maintain effective food plots properly. You'll also learn what types of plants deer prefer. Building food plots and improving the deer habitat on your land can be a source of pride, but you don't have to take my word for it. In fact, Neil advises to prepare for habitat improvement addiction: "I've helped hundreds of guys with their properties. Some of these guys are wealthy men who've built business empires. But they get started working on their property, making the habitat better, helping the deer along and that's all they can talk about. I see it over and over; this stuff is like a disease. It just gets in your blood!"

Habitat and Food Plot Pros

Much of the information and many of the photographs in this section of *Whitetail Quest* appear thanks to the expertise of the father-son team of Craig and Neil Dougherty. They offer habitat management workshops at their NorthCountry Whitetails Demo Center in Steuben County, New York. For more personalized services, you can also hire them to visit your land and help you design a comprehensive habitat improvement plan that will help you meet your deer hunting goals. For more information, write NorthCountry Whitetails, Dept NAH-B, 700 North Main Street, Newark NY, 14513; call (315) 331-6959; visit www.northcountrywhitetails.com; or e-mail info@northcountrywhitetails.com.

Don't Skip the Lime

Soil pH is a measure of the soil's acidity based on a 0 to 14 scale, with 7 being "neutral." Simply stated, a soil pH of 5 is 10 times more acidic than a soil pH of 6, and 100 times more acidic than a soil pH of 7. When the pH isn't at the optimum level for forage growth—6.5 to 7—plants literally cannot absorb the available nutrients from the soil (see chart below). Therefore, achieving a pH level of 6.5 to 7 by adding lime is more important than adding large amounts of fertilizer.

Most soils across the whitetails' range are acidic and require lime applications to neutralize. Only a few isolated areas, such as portions of Alabama's Black Belt region and some of the islands in the Mississippi River, have soils naturally above 7.

The most common form of agricultural lime is limestone rock ground almost to the consistency of powder, which is then spread by a commercial spreader (photo below). Pelletized lime can also be purchased in 50-pound bags and spread with a seed or fertilizer spreader. But pelletized lime costs about $200 per ton, while powdered lime costs only $15 to $35 per ton. Obviously, powdered lime is much more economical. When a soil test isn't available, 300 to 400 pounds of BioLogic's pHfertilizer per acre will supply the lime and fertilizer necessary for a great crop on most soils.

As a rule, lime should be applied at least a month ahead of planting to allow it to react with the soil. For perennial crops, however, timing isn't as important as applying enough lime to maintain proper soil pH. Lime is most efficient at neutralizing the soil's pH when it has maximum contact with the soil, so it's best

After you apply lime, use a disk to work it into the soil.

to disk the lime into the soil after it's applied. Also, soil moisture at the time of liming is important, since moisture is necessary for the lime's neutralizing chemical reactions to occur.

On most hunting properties, the acreage that can be developed into food plots is limited, so it's necessary to maximize the production of nutritious forage from these limited areas. Maintaining the appropriate soil pH of the food plots is an essential step to accomplishing this goal.—*Dr. Grant Woods, wildlife research biologist, BioLogic*

Applying lime to your food plot helps grow big bucks.

FOOD PLOT STRATEGIES

From seed to success.

BY SCOTT BESTUL

For Craig and Neil Dougherty, that autumn was a season to remember. The father and son team, owners of the consulting firm NorthCountry Whitetails (315-331-6959 or www.northcountrywhitetails.com), harvested three memorable bucks from their 500-acre hunting area in southwest New York. Most important to this story, however, is that the bucks were killed as they visited food plots the Doughertys had established.

"The first buck came in on the last day of the archery season," Neil recalled. "I was sitting on a small food plot I'd hunted only a few times all season—I'd purposely stayed away from it until the timing was right. The weather was cold and nasty, and I'd been on stand for a couple hours when a beautiful 9-pointer barreled into the field and just started gorging himself on brassicas! When he paused, I blew my grunt call, and he came in for a 10-yard shot.

"The next day was the shotgun opener," Neil said. "Bucks were still in rut, so I decided to stay with the food, knowing that's where the does would be. That evening I was sitting near one of our food plots when a small group of does entered, followed by a beautiful 10-pointer. I knew that buck well, having passed on a shot at him the year before. He'd put on close to 20 inches of antler in one season, and when he gave me a broadside 100-yard shot, I was able to take him."

Not to be outdone, Craig waited until the season's bitter end to prove "father knows best" by bagging a 154-inch 10-pointer. This December muzzleloader kill was extra special because Neil had found the sheds from the 5½-year-old buck the previous two years.

Success stories like the Dougherty's are becoming more common as hunters look for deeper involvement in their sport. Planting food plots not only benefits deer and improves the overall habitat for all species of wildlife, it's also a way for landowners to improve their hunting dramatically.

GROUND WORK

Neil stressed the importance of obtaining and testing soil samples. The time spent identifying, preparing and constructing a food plot is wasted if no seeds grow on the site, and one reason many food plots fail is improper soil treatment beforehand.

"The $10 or $20 it costs to obtain an accurate soil sample is the best money you'll ever spend if you want your food plots to succeed," said Dr. Grant Woods, a nationally known wildlife research biologist who developed Mossy Oak's BioLogic. "It will tell you what nutrients your soil might be lacking, which will then give you an idea of the fertilizer required to increase fertility. Soil tests also identify the relative acidity of your soil so you can apply the appropriate amount of lime. Most plants grow best in soils with a pH of 6.5 to 7, and the average pH level nationally is only 5.2."

Once the recommended amount of lime has been disked into the soil, fertilizer is used to increase soil nutrients and maximize plant growth, according to Woods. "The type of plant growing

On small plots, seeding and fertilizing can be done by hand.

example, 100 pounds of 6-12-12 fertilizer will consist of 6 pounds of nitrogen, 12 pounds of phosphate and 12 pounds of potassium. The remaining 70 pounds is filler, like sand.

The fertilizer should be disked 2 to 5 inches into the soil—the future root zone of your seeds. Once the fertilizer is disked into the soil, you can immediately begin sowing seed.

According to Woods, hunters who fertilize and plant during the spring should consider fertilizing again during late summer or early fall. "Forage-type crops like clovers use up nutrients from the soil as they grow," he said. "Spreading fertilizer on top of the plants a month or so before the hunting season will cause new plant growth and attract more deer to your plots. But don't spread fertilizer on plants during a drought. Adequate moisture is needed or your plants will 'burn' with the additional application."

For landowners with little experience maintaining food plots, the thought of driving an ATV or farm tractor over a beautifully growing field of deer food to spread fertilizer is a bit scary. "Don't worry about harming or killing the plants by driving over them," Woods said. "Again, unless you've had a drought, the plants are resilient."

in a plot the previous year influences the amount of nutrients required. For example, seed-head crops such as oats, wheat, rye and corn tend to deplete the soil of nitrogen. If you're planting a field where one of these crops previously grew, you'll likely need to fertilize.

"Conversely, legumes like alfalfa, clover and soybeans 'fix' nitrogen in the soil and are less likely to require it. However, they use a lot of phosphate and potassium. In fact, if you add nitrogen to such soil, all you're doing is helping weeds and grasses out-compete your food plot. That's why a soil test is needed to determine exactly what fertilizer blend is required to maximize plant growth on a specific site."

When you look at a bag of fertilizer, you'll notice a numbering scheme such as 10-10-10. These numbers refer to the amounts of nitrogen, phosphate and potassium in the fertilizer. For

Jack And The Beanstalk?

Know this: Despite advertising claims by marketers, there's no one seed that's going to grow well and be a deer magnet in every region of North America. Many folks planting their first food plots do so with their expectations beyond reality. In such instances, the chances for disappointment are excellent. Crops fail, or grow poorly, and your whitetails might ignore the same hotshot seed blend that your friend's deer, living only three states away, eat like candy. Or, as one industry expert pointed out, "We get a bumper crop of acorns one fall and I get guys calling me to say my seed doesn't work. It does work, but nothing you plant is going to pull deer away from white oaks. There are no 'magic beans' out there."

So what should you plant? Woods offers the following advice: "Finding the proper seed, or seed blend, can take some experimentation and time. I frequently tell people the best advice comes from those with dirt under their fingernails: local farmers and extension agents who make their living getting things to grow in your area. Talk to them, tell them what you're trying to accomplish and then follow their advice. Overall, I think planting alternating strips of different crops and seeing what grows well and what deer like is often a better approach than planting an entire field in one seed and hoping for the best."

Another piece of sound advice comes from Steve Scott of the Whitetail Institute of North America. As vice president of the oldest company devoted to food plots and whitetail nutrition, Scott has worked with curious hunters for years. "Many of the top companies, those whose entire business is food plot seeds, offer customer consultation for little or no cost," he said. "At the Institute, we have an agronomist and a biologist working for us full time, and they're more than willing to consult with hunters wanting to find the best plant types for their area. Through the years there isn't much we haven't dealt with, and we live by the motto, 'The only dumb question is the one you don't ask.'"

SELECTING SEED

All plant types can be divided into two categories: annuals and perennials. Annuals are plants with shallow root systems that grow for one season and then die. Some well-known examples of annuals are corn, soybeans, wheat and rye. Perennials are plants that establish a deep root system, flourish during the summer growing season, go dormant for winter, then repeat the cycle. Clovers and alfalfa are popular examples of perennials.

Deciding between annuals and perennials is largely a function of your goals for the plot itself. "In my experience, there are two types of food plot guys," Woods said. "Those who want to plant green stuff just so they can kill deer come fall, and those who want to improve the nutrition for their deer herd. So I view food plots as mission-specific. I can make a little quarter-acre 'hidey-hole' in the woods into a great place to kill a deer by just broadcasting a little seed during late summer, but I

For the overall health of the deer herd, landowners should plant both perennials, like clover, and annuals, like the brassicas shown here.

don't confuse that spot with a larger one where deer can come during the winter and get the nutrition they need. Naturally, you can have both types of plots on one property, but generally you'll plant different types of seed in each."

For many nutrition plots, a mix of annuals and perennials is typically the best bet. "Generally, we advise putting perennials in for the base," Scott said. "And that usually means clovers. The reason is they're the first things to green up during the spring, when deer need them the most. Lactating does need quality feed so they can nurse their fawns, and bucks require a high-protein diet so they can put on antler mass. Spring and summer feed is critical for these reasons, and in most areas, clover is the best answer." Scott notes there are many varieties of clover, and a variety that flourishes in the South might fail in more Northern climes, which is yet another reason to consult the expertise of companies with proven track records before selecting a variety.

Woods echoes this advice: "If you go into your local feed store, they're happy to sell you clover, but it's VNS (variety non-specific), the cheapest deal on the commodities market they can find. You want what's right for your area, and don't be afraid to pay a little extra for it. When you've gone to the trouble to construct and prepare a food plot, the difference in price between seed costing $20 per acre and $40 per acre is negligible.

Where It All Began

Proof positive that food plots work. These fine Alabama bucks were harvested on the Scott's hunting lease.

When Ray Scott (of Bass Anglers Sportsman Society fame) founded the Whitetail Institute of North America, it was based on a personal desire to improve whitetail hunting on the land he and his sons Wilson and Steve lease south of Montgomery, Alabama. What he discovered launched an industry that's revolutionized the way many serious deer hunters manage their hunting property.

"We leased land here and there and by 1975 had a pretty good-sized lease," said Steve Scott, vice president of Whitetail Institute. "Like most guys, we were looking for a simple plan to get the deer out of the woods so we could harvest them. Dad started looking at it a little bit differently, as he's always had a tendency to do.

"One year he planted clover and strips of various cereal grains to see how deer would react to them," Steve said. "To make a long story short, we routinely saw deer walk 50 to 100 yards through the cereal grains to get to the clover. It happened over and over.

"And not only did we see more deer, but over the years we began seeing better quality deer on those food plots. Dad wanted to know why, so he contacted an agronomist at Auburn University—Dr. Wiley Johnson, whom he later hired as director of forage research—and discussed the nutritious benefits of clover. So I give the credit to Dad as the one who started exploring the nutritional value of clover as a food supplement for deer and for acting on it. That's pretty much how our business started."

Ray's method would be to research and test every product thoroughly for effectiveness before it reached the public. And not just under controlled conditions, but in real-life situations on wild, free-ranging deer. Imperial Whitetail Clover, the Institute's first groundbreaking product, was subjected to seven years of testing and would set the stringent standard for the research and development of all future company products.

"The interest in what we're doing management-wise is skyrocketing," Steve said. "And rightfully so. Basically, there are two ways to kill a big buck: pay to go to some faraway place, or grow them on your own property. Many people are finding it's more rewarding to do it at home. People realize that if they plant quality food plots, practice good management and exercise restraint they can kill the biggest deer in their neighborhood."

Research remains the focus at the Institute. It currently has more than 15 different research projects in the works, and it's always in tune with the wants and needs of deer hunters and deer managers everywhere thanks to its network of field testers and the consultants who are in touch with hunters on a daily basis. There's always room for improvement, a philosophy the Whitetail Institute staff embraces. —*Gordy Krahn*

I'm also a big fan of blends, because if you've got five or six different types of seed out there and some stress factor (heat, drought, cold) comes along, it's probably not going to get all of them."

Planting a good-sized field in alternating strips of annuals and perennials creates a veritable whitetail salad bar, ensuring whitetails will have an attractive food source throughout the season. Perennials (like clover) green up early and are palatable to deer during spring and summer, but as perennials begin to go dormant (and their attraction to whitetails wanes) during fall, the annuals are coming into their own and become the draw.

Why don't deer hammer annuals as they grow adjacent to perennials? Because in many instances, annuals aren't palatable to (or preferred by) whitetails in their early stages of growth. Brassicas, for example, are a popular annual for whitetail food plots. Until they mature, however, many brassicas taste bitter to deer and are rejected. But once they "ripen" and cool weather arrives, starches in the plant turn into sugars and whitetails prefer them. For an analogy, consider corn. As an annual plant, corn is largely ignored by deer until the kernels reach maturity.

Because annuals mature quickly and frequently remain green well into the fall, they're an excellent choice for small hunting plots, such as the "hidey-hole" spots Woods referred to earlier. When incorporated into the larger feed plots with perennials, Woods will plant annuals closest to the forest edge where they'll be an attractant to deer when hunting season opens.

As a general guideline, Woods says 30 percent to 35 percent of your food plot acreage should be devoted to annuals, with the rest to perennials. One possible exception is in heavily farmed country. "There's no way your little food plots are going to compete with big fields of corn, soybeans and alfalfa on adjacent properties," Woods noted. "In that situation, I want a bunch of something

Once cool weather arrives, deer feed heavily in plots planted with brassicas.

that's getting green when those crops are harvested and the hunting season is on. Then, annuals are the way to go." In other words, let the farmers feed the deer all summer; you should feed them during the fall.

SOWING SEED

As generations of farmers have learned, timing is everything when planting a crop. Here again, talking to folks with "dirt under their fingernails" will reveal the best times to plant in your area to avoid moisture, heat and cold extremes that could inhibit plant growth.

"Generally, throughout this country you can plant during either the spring or fall and be successful," Scott said. "The exceptions would be the extreme North—where the short growing season requires spring planting—and the extreme South—where hot, dry summers make fall planting the best. The general guidelines we follow for the North are April 1 to June 15 for spring plantings and July 15 to August 20 for fall crops. In the South, the planting dates are February 15 to March 1 and September 1 to November 15."

Unless your food plots are large, you won't need heavy equipment to spread seed. "Anything less than 2 acres can be planted by one person walking with a simple broadcast spreader," Woods said. "They're an awesome tool. The trick is getting the proper coverage. I like to put about half the recommended seed (manufacturers provide coverage guidelines with their product) in the broadcaster and have it set on the smallest possible setting. I walk the field in one direction (east to

Creating a Wildlife Buffet

Whitetails aren't the only benefactors of food plots. In fact, game birds like pheasants, wild turkeys and quail respond as well as deer to a carefully managed food source. That's the belief of Wildlife Buffet's Dean Mierau, who loves to chase ringnecks and turkeys when he isn't waiting for whitetails. "The beauty of game bird food plots is you can do them on a small scale and still be productive, even in agricultural areas," Mierau said. "You'd be amazed at what you can accomplish on a ¼- or ½-acre plot."

As with whitetails, the key to game bird food plots is location. "With pheasants, for example, I like to place the plots as close to existing nesting, loafing or winter cover as possible," Mierau said. "With turkeys, I place food plots near traditional roosting trees. Upland birds that have to travel long distances to food are exposing themselves to danger, and you want to eliminate that travel for them if you can."

Similar to many whitetail food plot products, game bird seeds typically come in a blend. "In our 'Ringneck Ranch' seed, we have a mix of millet, buckwheat and other grains, as well as sunflower and peas," Mierau said. "Just like a deer food plot, you want to have high-quality food ripening at the time when upland birds need it most and it's most attractive to them."

One unexpected benefit to planting upland bird food plots is whitetails will also use them. I know this from personal experience. One August, I planted a ¼-acre plot of Wildlife Buffet's "Turkey Town" and a similar-sized plot of the company's "Buck Fall" beside it. The turkey blend (a perennial that includes both clover and alfalfa) drew turkeys as advertised, but also deer—lots of deer! In fact, one of my most productive early season bowhunting stands was positioned to ambush whitetails as they fed in the turkey plot. By early November, the deer started hammering the brassicas contained in the "Buck Fall" plot, but they never abandoned the turkey plot.

For more information on Wildlife Buffet products, call (888) 258-7413; or go to www.wildlife-buffet.com. —*Scott Bestul*

west) back and forth until I've covered it all. Then I put the remainder of the seed in the spreader and walk perpendicular to my previous direction (north to south) and spread the rest." Larger fields can be seeded with a broadcast spreader mounted to or pulled behind an ATV or tractor.

Once the seed is down, resist the temptation to run over it with implements that might bury it too deep. "One of the most common mistakes I see is people trying to bury the seed," Woods said. "These plants can't produce energy unless they get to see the sun. I'd rather have the seed lie on top of the soil and get driven in by the rain than have it buried alive. In fact, I plant my own food plots while it's raining because that way I'm guaranteed good seed-to-soil contact."

Scott concurs: "Imagine tapping on the seed with your fingertip—proper seed depth in the soil doesn't require any more force than that. A roller pulled behind an ATV or a cultipacker (a farming implement resembling a long hair-curler with ridges) pulled by a tractor are excellent ways for finishing the plot after seeding with clover."

ground. This allows you to compare how well different plants are growing in your plot, as well as how heavily deer are utilizing each variety."

Once established, a perennial food plot will produce literally tons of forage during the course of its life, provided it's maintained properly. "One of the biggest challenges with clovers, for example, is to keep them mowed so they maintain palatability to deer and are producing the maximum amount of nutrients," Neil said. "Any time your clover plot is at 40 percent to 50 percent bloom, it's time to mow."

Scott agreed, "If your deer population is high enough, you might not have to mow your clover. However, if deer densities are low, the food plot is large enough or other food sources simply keep the pressure off your food plot, you'll need to mow to help it along."

To guarantee proper mowing, Neil recommends using a rotary mower with sharp blades to ensure a clean cut and minimal damage to the plant. "Keep your mower's speed (rpm) high and your actual speed down," he said. "You want to cut

PLOT MAINTENANCE

Assuming you've prepped the soil correctly and the weather cooperates, your newly planted plots should start greening up in a few weeks. Time to ignore them and get ready for hunting season, right? Not so fast, says Woods. "As soon as I plant my seeds I erect utilization gauges in each plot. These are small cages that won't let deer eat the plants and shows you how they're growing minus the effect of deer browse. You can make a utilization gauge from a 10-foot section of 4-foot-high, ungalvanized (galvanized wire can inhibit plant growth) hog wire fence bent in a circle and staked into the

A small cage will show the effect of deer browse on your food plot.

Protecting Your Plots

At the annual Shooting, Hunting and Outdoor Trade Show (SHOT Show) I learned about the Plot Saver, an innovative food plot product I'm excited to try this spring. The Plot Saver is a repellent/fence system hunters can use on small food plots to protect them from overbrowsing by deer during the critical early stages of plant growth. The repellent, called Deer Stopper, was first developed in 1988 in New Jersey by Jim Messina, a landscape architect and nursery owner, to help his clients fight deer damage. The completely organic repellent keeps deer away by smell and taste, and it's not harmful to people, pets or wildlife that come in contact with it.

The system is easy to use. "After planting, position the Plot Saver fence posts around your plot," Messina explains. "Next, string the ribbon through the fence posts at a consistent height of 30 inches, then treat the ribbon with Deer Stopper. The repellent will be effective for 30 days, so if you need additional time to protect your plot, simply reapply it. After 20 minutes the treated ribbon will be dry and rainproof."

Messina says the Plot Saver works based on the deer's acute sense of smell: "If there's no deviation in the ribbon height, those deer

With the Plot Saver fence system in place, the left half of this field avoided overbrowsing by deer.

brave enough to approach the plot will quickly decide to find another food source because the smell will seem to be throughout the roped-in area."

J. Guthrie, managing editor for the Quality Deer Management Association, also sees the potential for this product. "Most wildlife biologists would never consider planting alfalfa or soybeans in their food plots unless they were several acres in size," he says. "This technique might open this category of highly preferred plants to deer managers with smaller food plots."

For more information on the Plot Saver, call (888) 411-3337; or go to www.plotsaver.com.
—Dave Maas

your clover fine and mulch it down into the plot to encourage regrowth. Don't 'wind-row' it, as the dense mats will choke out existing clover and allow weeds to grow. I recommend cutting clover down to 6 to 8 inches in height, so you're removing only one-third of the total plant height. It's rare to have to do this more than two or three times per growing season."

If your food plot blend contains both clovers and brassicas, mow the clovers to 6 to 8 inches, but once the slower-growing brassica plants reach this height, change the mower height to cut about 2 inches above the brassicas. In other words, never mow the brassicas. Instead, allow them to grow to increase the tonnage of food produced for the fall and winter season.

WEED CONTROL

Grasses and broadleaf weeds can choke out perennials, making the plot less attractive to wildlife and shortening its life span. "Grasses will usually show up during the second year of a perennial plot," Neil said. "Jump on them immediately. I

throughout the plot."

Neil says another option is to apply an application of Roundup using a hand sprayer or dispersed by a process called "wicking." "Weed-wicks are commercially available or can be constructed with any absorbent material," he said. "Saturate the wick with Roundup, then suspend it from the bucket of a tractor or the rear rack of an ATV about 6 inches above the food plot. By driving through the weeds, you'll apply Roundup without damaging any of the desirable plants below. It's important to apply the proper amount of Roundup and check the weed-wick frequently. If you apply too much Roundup to the wick, it will drip into the food plot and kill the very plants you're trying to grow. Not enough Roundup and you won't get the coverage you need."

While these treatments might seem like overkill, Neil notes they're far cheaper—and less time-consuming—than replanting. "With proper maintenance and some creative use of herbicides, you can extend the life of a perennial plot from the typical three to five years to more like seven to

Neil and Craig Dougherty with the results of good food plot management.

recommend a grass-specific herbicide like Poast. Apply it using product coverage recommendations for your plot size using a sprayer and an ATV. The entire plot will 'shut down' for about a week, but when the clover starts coming on again, it will eventually choke out the grasses and you'll be back in business. About two to three weeks after spraying, mow half the plot, then come back and mow the remaining half a couple weeks later. That keeps at least half the plot attractive to deer. I don't want them coming to my field and not finding something desirable to eat."

Broadleaf weeds (such as burdock, thistle, goldenrod, daisies and Queen Anne's lace) require more aggressive treatment. "One option is to let them get to within a week or so of going to flower, then mow off the tops," Neil said. "This will prevent them from going to seed and spreading

Periodic mowing helps clover plots produce the maximum amount of nutrients.

10 Steps to Building a Hunting Plot

1. Create the space through logging and/or bulldozer work.

2. Kill weeds if necessary, plow, disk and take a soil sample.

3. Hang treestands or build ground blinds near plot site.

4. Apply lime per soil test result, then disk it in.

5. Apply fertilizer and disk it in.

6. Broadcast seed. Roll plot if desired, but don't bury seed more than ¼ inch deep.

7. Set up utilization gauge (cage) and pray for rain.

8. Mow food plot—except brassica plants—to stimulate new growth.

9. Control grasses with Poast and broadleaf weeds with Roundup.

10. If desired, apply fertilizer one month before deer season.

On larger food plots a small farm tractor is invaluable.

ten years," he said.

As a perennial plot matures, Scott recommends soil-testing it each year to determine if additional applications of lime and/or fertilizer are needed. "And I just keep an eye on the field to determine its attractiveness to deer," he said. "If it seems like the plot has run its course, I till it up and plant an annual for a season, then start the process again."

Scott also encourages landowners to keep a detailed log of plant growth in each plot, as well as the dates/amounts of lime and fertilizer applications. "As time passes, you'll start to notice patterns so you'll know exactly how to treat certain fields and what grows best in them."

REALISTIC EXPECTATIONS

So you're blessed with a green thumb, and your newly established food plots are sprouting vegetation like some science experiment gone awry. Congratulations are in order, but keep your excitement in check. "Expect improvements, but not miracles," Scott advised. "You can have the best food around, but if your hunting land is in Florida, you aren't going to grow 300-pound deer. But you can help your deer reach their true potential.

"During your first season, you should see increased numbers of does and consequently, more buck activity than in the past. On a larger property where you can control a deer harvest, the second year should produce fewer spike and forkhorn bucks and better antler growth in 2½ year-olds. By the third season, bucks should really start growing impressive antlers due to the improved nutrition."

And further down the road? It's all dependent upon your hunting practices, your willingness to manage your land for better habitat and the potential of the deer themselves. Improving the nutrition and age structure in your deer herd is a complex mixture of variables that takes time, patience and commitment to achieve. But if you believe that success is a journey, not a destination, you'll be on the right path. And you'll no longer be just a deer hunter, you'll be a deer manager.

Something Out Of (Almost) Nothing

D r. Grant Woods has worked with deer hunters/landowners across the country, but he had his hands full when a hunting club with property in the Adirondacks hired him to make their place better. "They had 3,000 acres, but it was a mess," Woods recalled. "It was mostly mature timber, which is poor deer habitat. Nutrition was so poor that does were aborting fawns during a tough winter. The club members killed every buck they saw and never a doe. There were rumors of a 2½-year-old buck, but that was about it."

Woods talked with the hunting club members to get a sense of their commitment, then suggested a multi-pronged scheme. First, they'd implement a logging plan that would create large openings (10-plus acres) where the sun would reach the forest floor and allow trees and brush to regenerate. This would establish cover and feeding areas—a huge improvement in habitat. Second, winter deer feeding would stop and food plots would be planted to improve nutrition. Finally, no bucks would be harvested for several seasons to allow the age/herd structure to improve, but does would be shot. "This final suggestion was hard medicine for some of them to swallow," Woods said. "But they turned out to be a pretty remarkable group of guys. In fact, they haven't shot a buck in 6 years."

Establishing food plots wasn't easy, either. "There isn't a place on that entire acreage where you can sink a shovel 8 inches deep," Woods said. "The pH was 4.1 on some plots, so we had to put tons of lime down. The first year we took the 'easiest' 9 acres we could find and worked it up and planted it using ATVs. After that, they bought a small tractor and used it to clear and work log decks and other openings." Woods' goal was to have 1 percent (30 acres) of the land in food plots,

which has since been achieved.

The club's perseverance has paid off. "Their food plots are picture-perfect now, and the health of the deer herd has improved dramatically," Woods said. "Within a couple years, the fawn survival rate increased and the weight gains on these deer were unbelievable. Another barometer was the yearling buck activity, which went through the roof. Now these guys are seeing bucks they'd have considered trophies a couple years ago ... and they're letting them walk! It took incredible dedication and hard work, but if those guys can make it happen in that tough country, it's possible most anywhere."—*Scott Bestul*

Opening up the forest and its canopy is key to creating successful food plots.

The Tools of the Trade
By Tom Fegely

Craig Dougherty refers to his arsenal of farming machinery and implements as "big toys for big boys," pausing before thoughtfully adding "and girls." He knows first-hand the biggest investment in their business—habitat improvement for deer—is an arsenal of agricultural items ranging from tillers to tractors and ATVs. Add to that an array of implements including sprayers, spreaders, mowers, rollers, plows, cultipackers and more, and there's an investment amounting to big bucks even before the first big buck is harvested.

A small tractor is a godsend on larger plots.

The addition of deer-enticing food plots large and small on hunting leases and private grounds across much of North America has grown into a serious business in the deer hunting world. Although learning the cost of an initial investment in machinery and implements might at first discourage those wishing to embellish their hunting grounds with fields of brassicas, cow peas or clover, not everyone requires as many "big toys" as the Doughertys. After all, Neil and Craig own about 500 acres, while most landowners have considerably less.

The good news is most hunters interested in creating food plots can do the job with a modest investment or, for some, little more than the cost of seed and fertilizer alone. It all depends on the sizes of the plots and the amount of work necessary for converting weed fields or woodlands into scattered patches of supplemental forage. The more and bigger the plots, the more and bigger the machinery and implements required. However, some ultra-tiny plots that might catch a deer's interest don't require the use of any gas-powered implements except, perhaps, an ATV to carry seeds, rakes, fertilizer and other gear into some hard-to-reach places.

Simplicity For Starters

The first "mini food plot" on my 34 acres of southeastern Pennsylvania woodland was created with a leaf rake, a garden rake and a handheld herbicide sprayer on a tiny patch of sun-dappled woods near my favorite treestand. A couple weeks after spraying the area with Roundup to kill all existing vegetation safely, my wife and I spread lime and fertilizer, raked and re-raked the patch to loosen the soil, then hand-cast miniscule clover seeds across the 200-square-foot clearing. Then we barely covered the seeds by dragging the seeded area with leaf rakes. We completed the job by walking atop the plot to compact the soil and seeds.

That was followed by a more energetic yet equally frugal project the following spring. A ¼-acre opening was exposed to sunlight when a giant tulip tree and several smaller maples,

To break gound for tiny woodland food plots, a rake or rototiller is often sufficient.

To effectively kill weeds on a food plot, nothing beats an ATV-mounted sprayer with a wide boom attachment.

oaks and beeches blew down during the tailwind of a September storm. After some chainsaw work, a farmer-friend of mine spent a day clearing debris with his tractor, completing the job by scarring the humus with his tractor's bucket, readying it for planting. Clover seed was dispensed with a hand-operated seed spreader and a 4x6-foot section of chain-link fencing, which I dubbed the "poor man's harrow," was dragged behind my ATV to cover the seeds with a thin layer of dirt. A few more passes with the ATV sans the drag handily compressed the soil and seed, completing the task.

That year I also used my first mechanical aid for creating mini-plots: a garden-type Craftsman rototiller that eased the task of breaking the ground following the killing of existing vegetation with Roundup. The hand-guided rototiller chewed through 3-4 inches of soil, and in two passes broke up the clumps enough for raking and smoothing. Although the rototiller worked well on the small plots and trail edges, it's not a time-efficient way to work anything larger—leave that to the "big toys."

Tractor, ATV Or Utility Vehicle?

Size matters when it comes to determining how big, how many and just where to locate food plots to be created during a period of two or three years. The bigger the job, the bigger the investment and the heavier the machinery and implements. What's first on the shopping list? The initial purchase will either be a four-wheeler (ATV), one of the newer utility vehicles (UV) or a compact tractor.

• **TRACTORS.** For truly serious food plot builders, a compact tractor in the 35-55 horsepower range is arguably the best long-term investment.

A used compact tractor will run $3,000 to $8,000 or more at an auction or private sale, and considerably more if the unit is brand new, not including implements. If that's not feasible, you can still create large food plots by hiring a neighboring farmer with the proper implements for the project. Compared to doing the food plot work yourself, a farmer can often do it in a fraction of the time and cost. However, for many hunting clubs, creating food plots is part of the bonding process among members who look forward to weekend work parties at deer camp, taking pride in doing the job themselves to shape their grounds into high-quality whitetail habitat.

• **THE VERSATILE ATV.** If buying a compact tractor is out of the question, then consider an all terrain vehicle. The fast-growing popularity of planting supplemental deer foods has encouraged both agricultural supply and ATV manufacturers to create a line of accessories to satisfy nearly any food plot preparation chore. Keep in mind, however, that most implements made for tractors are typically too large and heavy for ATV use.

"Heavy implements might cause overheating on small, air-cooled ATVs," Craig Dougherty cautioned. "You can get a lot of work done with an ATV, but it's unrealistic to expect to plant 4- or 5-acre fields with ATV implements alone without putting in a colossal amount of time."

"Ninety percent of our clients are hunters, and most of them already own four-wheelers of some sort, which will save them money at the very start," said Neil Dougherty of the visitors to his food plot demonstration and deer management facility. "A 4WD, liquid-cooled ATV with a 400cc

Don't waste your money on cheap, lightweight disks. This model weighs more than 300 pounds and is built to take a beating.

engine is capable of making up to 3 acres of food plots a year, and I wouldn't recommend any unit that's much smaller."

As for ATV shopping, you'll find a plethora of manufacturers producing units tough enough for hunting and food plot work. Arctic Cat, Bombardier, Honda, John Deere, Kawasaki, Polaris, Suzuki and Yamaha offer plenty of choices (new and used) capable of doing the job. Your local ATV outlet, classified ads in the newspaper and agricultural periodicals and, yes, even eBay will help find used units for sale. For some clubs and leases, finding machinery to do the jobs might not be a problem because a few members already own them.

• **THE NEW UVS.** The newest ride on the farm and ranch scene is the utility vehicle (UV). These comfortable vehicles are able to perform a few of the planting chores such as pulling a mower, small disk or trailer-mounted seed spreader.

Food Plot Implements

Buying the right stuff for the job requires a bit of homework. A disk, for example, that's too light won't dig its teeth into hard soil sufficiently to create a seed bed. On the other end of the scale is the tractor disk that's too heavy for an ATV and will cause engine overheating.

So what's on the shopping list for the first-time food plotter? Here's an array of implements necessary for a start-to-finish project.

• **SPRAYER.** First on the food plot "must-have" list is a sprayer for dispensing the herbicide Roundup, which will rid the area of weeds and other unwanted vegetation. The Doughertys say a 25-gallon sprayer attached to an ATV will efficiently spray 1 acre without refilling. Their choice is the Monroe-Tufline ATV Sprayer marketed under the Mossy Oak BioLogic brand. The ATV mount is fitted with 10-foot spray booms that thoroughly wet the vegetation in a fan of liquid, plus a 15-foot hose and spray wand for tight spots or missed places.

• **PLOWS AND DISKS.** If you're installing food plots on land that's never been broken, a plow and compact tractor will probably be needed. You can buy used two-bottom plows for a couple hundred dollars. What's a "bottom?" It's the paddle that cuts into the ground. As a rule, you'll need a 20-hp tractor to pull a one-bottom plow, a 40-hp tractor for a two-bottom plow and a 60-hp tractor for a three-bottom plow.

Varied-width disks—preferably with serrated edges for efficient slicing into the soil—can be used on both tractors and ATVs, depending on their weights. With each pass, a disk turns up soil equal to its width. Prime time for disking is three to four weeks after spraying herbicide, unless dry weather conditions turn the soil into hardpan and plowing is necessary. Heavy, tractor-pulled disks might perform well under such conditions, but don't expect the lighter ATV disks to do the same. Chances are every tilling operation will require two or three passes to loosen the soil to 4 inches or more.

• **SPREADERS.** Putting down tons (literally) of pelletized lime or hundreds of pounds of fertilizer should be done with a well-built, pull-behind spreader. Lime and fertilizer needs, as determined by a soil sample, should be applied several weeks in advance of disking. If your food plots are accessible by truck, consider having a local agriculture supply store treat them with fine, pulverized lime.

• **ROLLERS AND CULTIPACKERS.** The final chore in bed preparation is to level the plot and cover the seeds with no more than ¼-inch of soil by

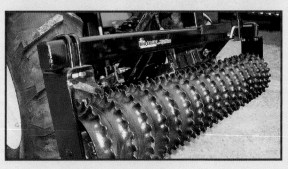

The right implement saves you time and increases the chance your food plot will be a success. From left to right: Cabela's ATV spreader, Tufline pull-behind spreader, John Deere mower, Tufline cultipacker and the Plotmaster, an all-in-one implement.

using a short-toothed lawn roller or some other device. On small plots, a water-filled lawn roller pulled behind an ATV works, as will a wood-framed section of chain-link fence pulled across the seeded plot.

A cultipacker is a dual-purpose food plot tool defined by one user as "a farming implement resembling a long haircurler with ridges." Cultipackers are rolled behind an ATV or tractor and do an efficient job of leveling and compressing the seed bed while providing good seed-to-soil contact for efficient germination.

• **MULTI-TASK IMPLEMENTS.** Dubbed by one writer as "the Swiss Army knife of implements," the Plotmaster from Woods-N-Water is worthy of the many praises heaped upon it. Pulled by an ATV or compact tractor, this all-in-one implement, available in 4-foot (for working tight woodland spots) or 8-foot models, performs the jobs of plowing, disking, planting and packing. All of the work is done in a single pass on suitable soils. Both manual and lift systems are available.

Wildlife Specialty's Brush Master Jr. serves the dual purpose of tilling, seed bed preparation, seed broadcasting and cultipacking all in a unit small enough for ATVs, but heavy enough to get the job done.

• **MOWERS.** The importance of mowing vegetation on land managed for deer and other wildlife isn't fully appreciated by many weekend farmers, says Neil Dougherty. Its purpose is to refresh the vegetative state of overly mature brush and abandoned fields or to trim a fast-growing clover crop.

The classic brush-eliminator is the rotary brush-hog, capable of trimming paths 5 to 20 feet wide when pulled behind and powered by a tractor of 50 hp or so. Next in line is the smaller (6 to 7 foot), self-powered, gas mower pulled by a compact tractor. For the ATV owner, however, the standard is a 4-foot mower capable of being pulled by larger 4x4s.

FIVE TOP HUNTING PLOTS

Not all food plots are created equal. Here's how to make yours better.

BY SCOTT BESTUL

As a growing number of whitetail hunters have embraced the notion of food plots, they've also recognized a cold, hard fact: Shooting deer in a poorly designed food plot is difficult. Whitetails can enter from unexpected (and often multiple) directions, making it difficult to plan an ambush, especially in large food plots. Once in a plot, deer feed heavily and often move little, making an undetected exit difficult for the hunter positioned near a field's edge. And sitting over a food plot repeatedly yields diminishing returns, because once deer know there might be a hunter nearby, they simply wait until dark to visit it. After multiple spookings, they might even quit dining there altogether.

Enter the hunting plot, a scaled-down version of a typical food plot designed to attract deer for a short time, funnel them so they can't detect a waiting hunter and position them for a shot opportunity. Neil Dougherty of Northcountry Whitetails (315-331-6959 or www.northcountrywhitetails.com) has spent the last several years perfecting the construction and use of hunting plots.

The use of hunting plots is a fundamental part of the Doughertys' success, according to Neil. "Hunting plots are distinguished from larger feeding or 'destination' plots in both size and purpose," he said. "We want deer to visit our large food plots and feel comfortable just putting on groceries. But the hunting plot is different. They're smaller in size and situated between bedding areas and a primary food source. Because hunting plots are small, deer don't spend a lot of time in them; they're almost viewed as a trip to the salad bar before they hit the main course. That's ideal for the hunter, because when shooting hours end you're not faced with the problem of getting down and busting deer. They've fed their way through and have moved on to the primary food source."

HUNTING PLOT BASICS

In general, hunting plots possess the following characteristics:

- They're ¼ to ¾ acres in size.
- They're situated between bedding areas and a major food source.
- They're constructed around an obvious stand site.
- They're planned with the prevailing winds of autumn in mind.
- They're designed to steer deer close enough to a stand/blind for a close shot.
- They allow a hunter to enter and exit a stand site without being detected by deer.

Neil has devoted countless hours to designing hunting plots, making unique adaptations to each using existing terrain and nearby cover. With that in mind, here's a look at Neil's five favorite designs, as well as his suggestions for where and when to use them.

THE SEE-THROUGH HOURGLASS

Neil's favorite hunting plot design, the Hourglass, has the unique ability to cover up to 1 acre of land, provide 10 tons of forage when planted with the proper mix of brassicas, clover and chicory, and steer deer within easy bow range. The Hourglass is an adaptable design that can be fit into many wooded or brushy areas and has accounted for many harvests.

"The Hourglass is effective because of how deer understand danger," Neil said. "While a deer often enters a field at a corner, it rarely stays there for long because it wants to immediately get to a point where it can see the whole field. So a deer will enter the Hourglass at one of the 'bulbs,' but the first thing it will do is start feeding toward the 'neck' or funnel near the center. To accomplish this you have to construct the plot so deer can see the field doesn't end at the neck; they have to see there's more field there, which piques their curiosity to move toward the funnel. And, of course, that's right where the stand is situated." One of the most important features of the Hourglass is the distance across the neck should be no more than 25 yards, which is within the effective range of most bowhunters."

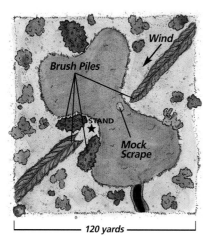

THE BOOMERANG BUSHWHACK

Similar in design to the Hourglass, the Boomerang is slightly smaller—usually a half-acre or less—making it easier to fit into tighter, thicker areas without removing as many trees. "Like the Hourglass, I pick the stand tree before I design a Boomerang," Neil said. "I find that stand tree by walking the cover between a destination food source—either a large feeding plot or even an oak flat—and look for an area where multiple deer trails converge. Deer will

accept and begin using your food plots more readily if you place them in areas where they already want to be."

The Boomerang works on much the same principle as the Hourglass, as deer feed toward its apex so they can see the entire field. Naturally, the apex is also the site of the stand. "When I have a bulldozer operator construct a Boomerang, I explain to him the importance of placing two windrows or piles of brush directly behind and in front of the stand," Neil said. "These prevent deer from entering the field downwind of my stand and busting me. I also like to have a logging road or other easy entry/exit trail that allows me to get to and from my stand without alerting any nearby deer."

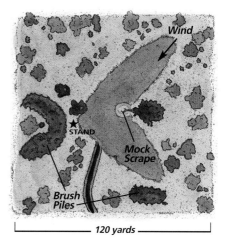

THE LONG SHOT 'S'

Designed with both the bow- and gun-hunter in mind, the Long Shot 'S' is most effective when placed in natural funnels and crossings, especially between two woodlots or existing fields. Typically, Neil keeps the maximum width of the Long Shot at about 20 yards, so feeding deer will be steered within bow range. But the length of the Long Shot can be extended as far as a hunter is willing to shoot with a gun, since the gentle curves of this plot still allow for a good view of most of the plot. Usually 150 to 200 yards is a good maximum length.

Despite its length, Neil makes the Long Shot an effective bowhunting plot by constructing a "bulb" at one end of it. "Usually the bulb is no more than 30 yards wide and situated near the best tree for bowhunting," Neil said. "I put brush piles downwind of the stand tree, then place mock scrapes and licking branches within shooting distance. Because the visibility is best at the bulb, deer will naturally want to congregate there and the mock scrapes will be a strong attractant for any bucks cruising through."

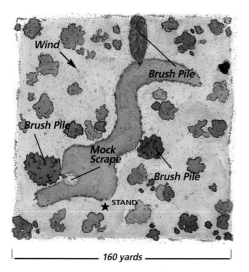

160 yards

THE COMFORTABLE CORNER

Neil's favorite design is another example of creating a food plot that capitalizes on the natural feeding behavior of deer. "It's well known that whitetails gravitate toward the edge created by two cover types," Neil said. "And they also like to feed near a corner that allows them to view the entire field for danger. This design contains both those features."

Like the Stakeout, the Comfortable Corner is a good fit for creating a hunting plot adjacent to an existing field. Ideally, the forage planted to this food plot will be peaking as the palatability of the existing field is diminishing. "As an example, you could plant the Comfortable Corner to brassicas, which deer will hit hard as cold weather comes," Neil noted. "And the existing field might have alfalfa, which will have lost much of its appeal by hunting season."

Creating the edge effect along the field is another key to making this plot work. Neil recommends increasing sunlight to the Corner by thinning trees for about 50 yards in all directions, taking care to choose stand trees before starting any chainsaw

work. The thinning process will cause the cutover area eventually to grow up to brush and young trees, making this an ideal staging area for deer before they enter the hunting plot. Again, if possible, create brush piles or windrows to steer deer away from the downwind side of your stand.

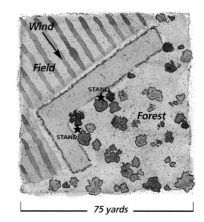

75 yards

THE STRIP STAKEOUT

The Strip Stakeout is a deceptively simple design with multiple applications. Placed between wooded cover and a destination plot, such as a farm field, the Stakeout can be constructed by bulldozing a brushy transition area to create a stopover hunting plot. It's also ideal for use on land that a hunter doesn't own. "If you don't have the time, money or land control to create a hunting plot, a farmer might agree to let you use 1/4 acre or 1/2 acre on the edge of an existing field for a food plot," Neil said. "That scenario is ideal for the Stakeout."

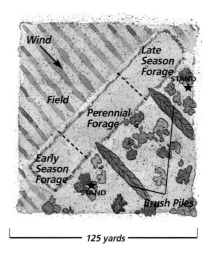

125 yards

Avoiding Five Food Plot Pitfalls

The following story is true. The man's name, however, has been changed for obvious reasons.

Last year Joe Arnold, a friend of mine, moved into a rustic house, one situated in the midst of a forest. Deer and turkeys were plentiful around his home, so Joe cleared out an area in the woods for a food plot. He worked the soil and planted it in white clover. Within two weeks Joe had the prettiest stand of clover he'd ever seen.

Knowing the plot needed fertilizer, Joe ventured to the local lawn and garden store. He wasn't there long before he saw what he needed—Miracle Grow fertilizer. He knew it was a great product because it had worked wonders for his wife's flowers. Rushing home, Joe applied the fertilizer to his plot and sat back to watch it grow. When he checked his plot a few days later, however, he was shocked to see his entire clover field was dead! Strangely though, the grass was growing well. Joe was crushed.

Puzzled, he found the fertilizer bag and read the instructions. He dropped his head in disgust. He'd used a great fertilizer, but one designed for fertilizing lawns. Listed on the bag was one of its strengths: killing unwanted white clover in grass!

Almost everyone who's planted food plots has had a "Joe experience." And for those of you reading this in anticipation of planting your first plot, I guarantee you, too, will make a few mistakes along the way. In the following five examples, I'll share some common food plot problems, what causes them and how you can avoid, or cure, each one.

Q: Although my crops are tall and lush during mid-summer, the deer don't eat them. Why?

A: My wife and I cut wild asparagus shoots during early spring and steam them in butter. They're delicious. When asparagus matures, however, it becomes tough and fibrous. The same thing happens to mature food plot plants. This is why it's important to mow clover, alfalfa and similar plants when they reach approximately 12 inches in height. Set the mower so it leaves plant stems approximately 7 inches high. In just a few days, you'll once again have tender shoots for the whitetails to feed on, and they'll immediately return.

Q: I planted a special clover blend in my first food plot. I worked the soil to perfection, applied plenty of fertilizer and quickly had a terrific stand of clover. Within weeks, however, plant growth in the plot came to a standstill. What did I do wrong?

A: In cases such as this, the all-important step of taking a soil test was skipped. It tells you the soil's pH, or "potential of hydrogen." It designates the acidity and alkalinity of the soil. A lower pH number means the soil is acidic, a higher number means it's alkaline. A pH number between 6.5 and 7 (neutral pH) is ideal. Because soils in most parts of our nation are too acidic, tons of lime need to be added to bring a soil's pH level up. Interestingly, a soil's nutrients are bound against the individual soil particles. The more acidic the soil is, the tighter the nutrients are bound. Therefore, in acidic soils the plants

This food plot will have grass problems because the vegetation wasn't killed with Roundup before plowing.

This is every food plot builder's dream—a lush field that benefits the deer and, ultimately, the deer hunter.

are unable to use the nutrients. They grow slowly, never reaching their full potential.

Having the proper pH is more important than applying fertilizer. Take a soil test and apply the correct amount of lime, then apply fertilizer.

Q: Why is it I can't grow grass in my yard, but it grows like crazy in my food plots?

A: Grass and weeds are a common food plot problem. Interestingly, when London, England, was first bombed during World War II, flowers that hadn't been seen within the city in centuries bloomed the following year. This occurred because the bombing unearthed seeds that had been buried deep within the earth for hundreds of years. Yes, flower seeds are durable, and so are grass and weed seeds. Here are the steps to take to keep grass and weeds to a minimum.

First, if any vegetation is present, mow the area to be planted. Leave the area alone for a couple days and then spray it with a herbicide such as Roundup or Ultra. This will kill the weeds and grasses. Seven to ten days later, plow or disk to work the dead matter into the earth. Break up the clods, and work the soil down to a smooth seedbed. Plant your product according to the instructions, and you'll have a relatively weed- and grass-free food plot.

As noted, weed and grass seeds are tough and do remain within the soil. When grass and weeds do appear, they must be treated.

Q: I don't have a lot of money to put into food plots. How can I best spend it?

A: A perennial product such as clover comes up year after year and will last five to seven years if the plot is properly cared for. To get more bang for your buck, plant your plot in early fall, mixing an annual fall attractant with your perennial seed. In the North, for example, you could plant oats with clover. The oats will come up and grow well and attract whitetails during November and December. Then the following spring the clover will take over and last for years. You might want to overseed the clover from time to time.

Q: I took a soil test, added lime and fertilizer, then worked my soil into a fine level field. I seeded my ground with an ATV-mounted spreader, then disked the entire plot. My stand of alfalfa is spotty at best. Why?

A: Like my friend Joe at the beginning of this article, this hunter didn't read the instructions on the bag. Alfalfa, clovers and some other seeds should be planted only ¼ inch deep. Disking pushes seeds such as this too deep, and many of them can't come up. Wheat, oats and rye, on the other hand, can be planted 1 to 1½ inches deep. For shallow planting seeds, broadcasting them just before a rainfall actually works very well. Always read the seeding instructions before you plant. —*Brad Herndon*

MICRO PLOTS FOR MACRO BUCKS

Luring big bucks to small food plots is easier (and more affordable) than you think.

BY TOM FEGELY

You need not be a land baron to enjoy the benefits of food plots. Even that 2-acre patch of woods behind your house or the 5 acres owned by Cousin Bart on the other side of the county might qualify as sites for white-tailed deer food plots.

The first time I heard the term "food plot" was during a hunt in Alabama more than 25 years ago. The term was then used inter-changeably with "green field." Today, green field suggests large, open acreage of anything from soybeans, rye and wheat to smaller plots composed of special-ized cultivars to suit the tastes and nutrition needs of deer and other game.

I enjoy deer hunting near food plots. On my visits to Dixie, I'd always spend the final hour or two of a day's hunt inside a shooting house on the edge of a 25- to 50-acre food plot where the chance for spotting a trophy buck grows as the light slips away.

A couple decades back, I lived on a 3-acre Pennsylvania woodlot, one-third of which was lawn and the remainder was deciduous woods of oak, maple, beech and tulip-poplar. Deer were

Armed with only hand tools, landowners can expose the forest floor to sunshine—a key to growing healthy micro plots.

seen regularly as they traipsed through my yard and woods on their way to surrounding corn, oat, wheat and soybean fields.

By the mid-1980s, commercial food plot popularity was just tak-ing root, although not much more than a succulent whitetail clover and other farm crops were available. So I stopped by a farmer-friend's home one April morning and stocked up on a few samples of white clover, rye and oats. With a minimum of soil preparation I scattered the seeds in a sunny spot, and within two weeks things were turning green. Deer tracks and droppings were soon found on my narrow 30-yard-long micro plot, which survived only into early summer when the canopy's foliage blocked out the neces-sary sunlight and drought issued the coup de grace.

So marked the beginning of my love affair with small food plots, free of misconceptions that my meager offerings would yield bucks with bigger antlers or hold deer from neighboring properties on a permanent basis. My sole purpose was to draw deer 12 months a year for viewing, photographing and, eventually, harvesting.

Today, my wife and I tend plots and hunt on the 35 acres surrounding our home that was purchased in 1997. Our hunting success has improved, as have the regular sightings of both whitetails and turkeys on the farm-and-woodlot property.

RECIPE FOR SUCCESS

Creating micro plots is a relatively easy and inexpensive task, provided you take the right steps.

• **SELECT THE BEST SITE.** Step No. 1 in creating micro-plots on your hunting property is finding the right spot for a treestand or ground blind. This, of course, varies dramatically from one woodlot to another depending on the landscape.

"My first choice would be a funnel area connecting two woodlots," advises Neil Dougherty. "Second, check out the prevailing winds and place your treestand accordingly."

Another key to choosing a viable site is looking for native grass growth on the woodland floor. If grass can grow, it's a good bet clover, chicory or other deer attractants will also have sufficient sunlight to grow. Forget about bare earth sites that might at first seem appealing—the lack of growth indicates insufficient sunlight.

• **TAKE A SOIL TEST.** Most soils are pH deficient, and chances are you'll have to add lime to each small plot to bring up the pH readings to at least moderate acidity (6 to 6.5). Even though the woodland soil might seem dark, moist and rich, that doesn't necessarily mean it'll support a new type of planting. Soil samples can be sent or taken to most university agricultural extension services, and some seed producers also sell test kits, usually for $10-$12 or less. A soil analysis will reveal the soil's pH and recommend the amount of lime and fertilizer to apply for specific

plants. No matter how small the tract, a soil test is mandatory.

• **PREPARE THE SOIL.** After one or more potential sites have been chosen and the soil tested, it's time for clearing grasses, weeds, saplings and intruding brush. Begin by raking dead leaves from the plot area, then get rid of the grass and weeds with a herbicide such as Roundup, which does the job in about a week. Using a herbicide is much more effective than cultivating, especially on small plots where ATVs or tractors are ineffective. After the vegetation has turned brown, hand-raking a smooth bed is recommended followed by the addition of lime and fertilizer.

The clearing operation is relatively simple compared to disking and cultivating and planting large tracts of field. It's made even more simple by "walking in" a garden tiller and string trimmer along with leaf and garden rakes, shovels, long-handled and short-handled tree pruners.

In addition, a tree or two with large canopies might need to be trimmed or chainsawed to allow for the necessary three to four hours of daily sunlight. Problem is, spring plantings are often done before the greening up of a woodland and shading increases as foliage grows. From mid- to late summer and into early fall, heavily-shaded areas are

A garden tiller does an efficient job of breaking up the soil and mixing in lime and fertilizer. It also saves muscle strain. If you don't own a tiller, beg, borrow or rent one.

obvious and shouldn't be planted.

• **MOW AND RESEED.** Ironically, thanks to the diminutive sizes of woodland food plots, success in attracting deer might create a problem if overgrazing occurs.

"Not only will deer sometimes eat everything there," Dougherty said, "but just their walking across the plot while eating might hinder the plot's ability to survive. This doesn't matter on large plots, but it can seriously affect small plots that have high moisture content. Reseeding might be required in such places."

This is one of the author's best hunting plots. It's planted in clover, and the exposed dirt area contains a mineral lick.

Dougherty also recommends mowing clovers and other cultivars as they mature, then reseeding and refreshing with more fertilizer. The reseeding should be done at the end of August, and no raking is necessary. A 35-40 percent germination rate can be expected.

• **PLAN YOUR AMBUSH.** Now that your micro plots are in place and growing, it's time to shift your attention to details that will carry your summer project to fruition. Placement or replacement of treestands or ground blinds is your next order of business. In the second year of residence on our 35-acre hunting grounds, my wife and I set both homemade wooden stands and portable commercial stands on our initial four plots. Except for one stand, the others were set within spitting distance of the clearings, which seemed reasonable at the time as the woods were in full foliage.

By early November, however, leaves began to fall and it became obvious our setups were too close to the clearings. Deer were quick to detect anyone in a stand. Even though the woods were largely leafless by mid-November, deer could easily be seen using the same approach routes they used during the early bow season. Most deer were shot before they worked their ways into the clearing.

Our final project began the following spring when we took on the task of planting the edges of an ATV trail bordering our holding. A farmer-friend helped us by scraping the grassy and brushy trail sides wherever sunlight had encouraged plant growth. We planted much of the area in clover,

which did quite well as it spread onto the trail on its own. No alterations or additional plantings were made in heavily shaded areas. Today, eight micro plots plus the openings exposed in clearing the ATV path total nearly 1½ acres of clearings in our whitetail woods.

For "dessert" we also place 3 or 4 mineral blocks and granular licks in several easy-to-view sites—one only 50 yards from my office window. The licks serve to lure and briefly hold deer on their passages across my woodlot. In some places, such as my home state of Pennsylvania, the licks must be removed a month prior to the fall bow season opener. Check your state game agency's regulations.

• **THINK SMALL.** The bottom line is you don't need vast acreage to establish productive food plots in your woods. As deer became accustomed to traveling between my tasty and nutritious food plots, they lingered longer before moving off to soybean, corn and wheat fields on bordering lands. My land always was a staging area of sorts, but with the addition of scattered food plots, deer now spend more time sampling the "fast food" we offer them. They spend more quality time on our land than ever before.

SECRETS OF THE FOOD PLOT EXPERTS

These seven insights, from those who know, will make your food plot experience easier and more successful.

BY TODD AMENRUD

Unfortunately, many novice land managers will have food plot failures this year. To make matters worse, the following year they'll go out and plant the same thing in the same manner and expect a different result. Yes, Mother Nature has her influences, but "know-how" is a critical component when it comes to food plot success. If you do things right, you can battle undesirable weather conditions for respectable food plots.

Trial-and-error is an expensive and time-consuming approach to this venture—I know from experience. Many years ago I was a stubborn, uneducated land steward and wasted a lot of time and money on things I believed would be good for my white-tailed deer herd. Some things worked, but many did not.

Very simply, it pays to listen to food plot experts—people who've "been there, done that." Here's your chance to learn from some of the best.

Plant the right seed in the right spot and your reward could be a close-range shot at a relaxed and well-fed buck.

1. TAKE THE FOOD TO THE DEER

According to Sherman Berry, habitat consultant for Mossy Oak/BioLogic, mature bucks are often hard to lure into a large agricultural food source during legal shooting light. "Those big guys seem to hang in the shadows and appear after dark," he said. "I suggest hunters bring the food source closer to whitetail bedding areas. Place your plots in areas where even mature bucks will feel comfortable feeding during daylight hours."

Berry classifies his plots as either "feeding plots" or "hunting plots." A feeding plot is relatively large and its purpose is to provide as much nutrition as possible to as many deer as possible. Berry doesn't hunt these plots.

A hunting plot is a smaller hideaway that gets at least five hours of sunlight a day, but also has great cover and bedding areas close by. An out-of-the-way spot like this allows mature bucks to feel more safe and sound during shooting hours.

2. HIT THE PLANTING WINDOW

Every year, Jeff Best, regional sales manager for Tecomate Wildlife Systems, talks to well-intentioned hunters and landowners who work very hard to prepare their planting sites. "They take all the appropriate steps, such as pulling soil samples,

The only thing the author enjoys more than building food plots is hunting over them.

spraying for weeds, tilling the soil, correctly applying lime and fertilizer, as well as preparing a firm seed bed," he said. "They do all this and then make the critical mistake of planting during the middle of a drought."

Best says the key to a successful food plot is doing all the above-mentioned activities and then waiting for an ideal "planting window." Planting too early or late, or in the wrong moisture conditions, will cost production—and maybe even the entire crop. "In the Upper Midwest the moisture issue seems to be more of a challenge during the fall planting season," Best said. "This doesn't mean you can't plant during the fall in this region. You can, but you need to wait until you have moisture in the ground."

3. FIND THE BEST LOCATION

With most successful businesses, location is a key factor. Likewise, site selection is a major contributor to your overall food plot success.

According to Dean Mierau, co-founder of Wildlife Buffet seed blends, you should develop a written plan for the location and design of your plots. "Your goal as a hunter/landowner should drive the site location," he said. "For instance, if you want to provide a late-season food source for deer, the plot should be adjacent to key deer wintering areas, thus minimizing deer travel times and energy expenditure. If you want to hunt directly over a plot, a significant amount of time

should be placed on site location to ensure access to treestands or ground blinds is possible without crossing game trails. In addition, prevailing winds must be considered so deer approaching the plot don't pinpoint your location."

4. CHOOSE A BLEND

Rob Echele, marketing manager for Purina Mills, says low-cost food plot seeds typically deliver poor performance. "Many inexpensive food plot offerings are agricultural-grade seeds such as milo or rye that are bred primarily for livestock consumption," he said. "You're much better off choosing a seed blend consisting of forage-grade cultivars, which means the seeds are bred specifically for consumption by deer. These blends were developed after many years of research and will perform much better than generic low-cost seeds. Consider this: Does it really matter how much money you saved on cheap seed if it doesn't grow well or deer won't eat it?"

Echele recommends planting a blend of several seed types, because plots consisting of just one type of seed (he calls them "mono plots") are generally at a much higher risk for failure. Why? Echele says if a mono plot experiences just one of these problems, it affects the entire plot because there's only one type of plant in the field. You're

For bucks to reach their maximum antler potential, they need highly nutritious food.

essentially putting all your eggs in one basket.

5. TEST YOUR SOIL

Land manager and habitat consultant Kurt Amundson gets to talk with many people about their food plot successes and failures. When trying to decipher the cause of the failures, he asks a lot of questions, many of which are tied to the results found in a soil test. Yet he's amazed at the number of times a landowner's reply is, "What soil test?"

Amundson says as a food plot builder, you need to know what you're up against so you know what to adjust to be successful. "Without taking a soil sample, you can only guess what to plant and if lime and/or fertilizer is needed," he said. "It's one of the most overlooked parts of the planting process, yet it'll save you more time and money than any other step."

Some first-time food plotters make the mistake of burying tiny seeds, such as clover, too deep with a disk for consistency. A good way to obtain solid seed-to-soil contact is by using a cultipacker.

option. If you have access to a cultipacker or some type of a roller, go ahead and use it, but remember: Don't cover the seed too deep."

6. DON'T KILL THE SEED

Kevin Small of KT's Outfitters manages 6,500 acres of private land for whitetails in northeast Missouri. "In the past I was guilty of wasting time, money and seed in building food plots," he said. "After working the soil, I'd broadcast seed and then cover it up by pulling a disk over the seeded area or using a homemade 'drag' of some sort. Little did I know I was burying the seed too deep."

Many of the seeds that grow some of a deer's favorite foods are so small you can fit them under your fingernail. People fail to realize seeds are living organisms, and a small seed such as a clover, brassica or chicory contains only a small amount of energy. The seed needs moisture to release that energy. If a tiny clover seed is buried more than approximately ¼ inch, it dies before it can reach the surface. Obviously, larger seeds, such as corn, contain more energy so they can be buried deeper.

"After years of frustration," Small said, "I learned that small seed needs to make contact with the soil—nothing more. If you've worked the soil by disking or tilling you don't need to do anything more after broadcasting the seed. The simple act of the soil settling will ensure good seed-to-soil contact. Planting before a rain is another effective

7. HAVE PATIENCE

Duane Domaszek, zoo owner and whitetail nutrition specialist, says many hunters get over-anxious and grab a bag of seed, rush into the woods and then broadcast it onto the ground. "Because they don't have a plan, these hunters will most likely not be satisfied with the results," he said. "You should consider your goals, budget, timeline and access to equipment before hastily heading afield."

Site evaluation is an important initial step. If you plan things correctly you can almost dictate to your whitetail herd where they're going to eat, sleep and travel. This makes it much easier when it comes time to hunt.

Domaszek says those who are in a rush should understand that being a whitetail manager and a land steward is an ongoing endeavor, and most goals aren't obtained overnight. "You do what you can now and then add to it as you go," he said. "With a plan and a healthy dose of patience, over time you can develop your own whitetail hunting paradise."

INDEX

rattling, 97

scent trails, 31–33, 97

stand placement and, 96–97

tending grunt, 97

trailing grunt, 99–100

transition zone strategy for, 96

weather fronts and, 103,
    105–106

Rut-hunting mistakes, 87–89

calling, 88

equipment, 89

hunting different areas, 89

hunting same sign too long, 87

hunting where you saw bucks
    last month, 88

not hunting all day, 89

not hunting doe pockets, 88

scent control, 88

shooting lanes, 89

thick cover and, 88

S

Scent-Blocker, 25

Scent bombs, 29, 34–35

Scent-control clothing, 24–25

Scent-Lok, 24–25

Scent posts, 33–35

key tips, 34–35

placing, 33–34

purpose of, 33

Scents

cover scent, 28

curiosity scents, 28

food scents, 28

masking scents, 28

sex scents, 28

territorial scents, 28

Scent Shield, 25

Scent strategies

activated charcoal, 25

applying scent to decoys, 35

backyard bucks, 61

doctoring scrapes, 37–41

importance of, 21–23

masking scents, 28–29

odor eliminators for boots and

clothing, 24

personal hygiene for, 23

putting clothing on, 23–24

as rut-hunting mistakes, 88

scent bombs, 29

scent-control clothing, 24–25

scent posts, 33–35

scent trails, 13, 31–33

sex-scent strategies, 29

storing clothing, 23

territorial scents, 29

Scent trails, 31–33

boot method, 32

drag rags, 32–33

rut-hunting, 97

tarsal gland method, 33

Scott, Ray, 130

Scott, Steve, 129, 130, 131, 133,
    136

Scott, Wilson, 130

Scouting

for backyard bucks, 60, 62

importance of, 68–69

for reality whitetail hunting, 73

Scrape hunting

doctored scrapes, 37–41

doe-in-estrus scent, 29

Scrapes

boundary, 96

mock scrapes, 32, 41

primary, 96

secondary, 96

Secondary scrapes, 96

See-through hourglass design,
    143–144

Sex scents

defined, 28

strategies using, 29

Shooting

passing up first good shot, 48

ready to shoot on opening day,
    81–82

slow-steady-spot-squeeze, 74

Shooting lanes

clearing, 89

Sighting-in guidelines, 75

Sitting still

beating boredom, 13

comfort counts, 12

hunting pressure and, 11

importance of, 9–13

mental game, 11

on opening day, 82–83

during rut, 11

slo-mo rule, 12

staying warm, 11

300-yard rule, 12

Slow-steady-spot-squeeze, 74

Small, Kevin, 155

Sneak-hunt, 110

Sneaky feet approach, 77–79

tips for walking through
    woods, 78–79

training eyes and mind for,
    77–78

Soil

acidity of, and adding lime,
    123, 125

preparing for food plots,
    122–123, 150

taking soil sample for food
    plots, 122, 123, 127,
    146–147, 150, 155

Sprayers, 140

Staging areas, 46

big bucks, 16

Stand placement

backyard bucks, 63

for big bucks, 15–19

close to beddng area, 18

confidence in location of, 11

farmland deer, 56–57

hunt travel corridors, 15–16

nocturnal bucks, 18–19

rut-hunting, 96–97

staging areas, 16

utilize choke points, 16–17

Stands. *See also* Stand placement

beating boredom, 13

comfort counts, 12

importance of sitting still, 9–13

setting up too soon, 46–47

Still-hunting

sneaky feet approach, 77–79